The Most Wonderful
Time *of* All Years

The Most Wonderful Time *of* All Years

A Christmas Reader *for the* Season *of* Advent

Darrell W. Johnson

Regent College Publishing
Vancouver, British Columbia

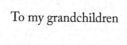

Published 2013 by Regent College Publishing
5800 University Boulevard, Vancouver, BC V6T 2E4 Canada
Web: www.regentpublishing.com
E-mail: info@regentpublishing.com

Regent College Publishing is an imprint of the Regent Bookstore <www.regentbookstore.com>. Views expressed in works published by Regent College Publishing are those of the author and do not necessarily represent the official position of Regent College <www.regent-college.edu>.

Cataloging in Publication information is on file at Library and Archives Canada.

ISBN 978-1-57383-496-4

All Scripture quotations, unless otherwise indicated, are taken from the New American Standard Bible®, copyright 1995 by the Lockman Foundation.

Contents

Introduction   9

Week One (Luke 1:26-56)   13
Week Two (Luke 1:1-25, 57-80; Matthew 1:1-17)   45
Week Three (Matthew 1:18-25; Luke 2:1-21)   80
Week Four (Luke 2:22-40; Matthew 2:1-23;
        Luke 2:41-52)   111

Christmas Day: If the Real Story Be Told . . .   144

The Most Wonderful Time of All Years

"It's The Most Wonderful Time of the Year."

I do not know all that Edward Pola and George Wyle had in mind when, in 1963, they composed the song made so well known (in the Western world anyway) by singer Andy Williams. But I do know that they chose the right word for the season in which we hear it sung: *Wonderful*. Full of wonder.

The Advent-Christmas season is the most "wonder filled" time of the year. Yes, it can also be the most "stress filled" time of the year – with so much to do. And for many, it can become the most "debt filled" time of the year – if we buy into all the advertising of the latest must-have toys and gadgets and experiences. And for others, it can be the most "sorrow filled" time of the year – when we painfully miss those who have gone on to the other side, whose presences were part of the wonder of past years. Yet in the midst of it all, the season is filled with wonder.

Ever since I was a young boy, Christmas, and the season of Advent leading up to it, has been my favourite time of the year. In late summer, as we begin to taste the fall air moving in, I begin to think about all that will be coming very soon. The lights on people's houses (while living in Manila, the lights on all the tall buildings downtown!), the smells wafting from kitchens and pastry shops, the sounds on the radio and on shopping mall PA systems, the gatherings with family and friends, the special times of worship, the gift giving inspired by the actions of the magi who came to adore the new born King. I can hardly wait!

But what finally makes the season so "wonderful" is the story we read and tell and sing, the story that has inspired more music and painting and intellectual grappling than any other in the history of the world, the story that fulfills the longings of so many of the stories that cultures have created to make sense of human life in this world. It is the most wonderful time of the year because of the most wonderful story ever told. And the wonder is: the story is true, so very true.

I have had the unspeakable privilege of preaching the story for over forty years now, and as I say each year, the story keeps getting richer and richer, deeper and deeper. I trust I will be granted the grace to preach it for many more years since it keeps opening up more and more wonder.

In this book I am inviting you to inhabit the story with me. The book is laid out in a daily devotional style, designed to help you live in the story over four weeks, the weeks of Advent leading up to Christmas. Each week begins on Sunday with a text from one (or more) of the four Gospels. On each of the following days, I offer you a reflection on the text. The reflections are portions of sermons that I have preached. At the end of each reflection is a prayer taken from others who have studied and told the story.*

In the first week, we enter the story through Mary, the mother of Jesus (Luke 1:26-56), with two days devoted to her experience of the wonder, and the following days listening to what she thinks are the implications of the birth of her son as she sings them in her Magnificat.

In the second week, we listen to what Zacharias, the father of John the Baptist, understands about the wonder (Luke 1:1-25, 57-80). We will take time to understand the genealogy of Jesus as given by Matthew (1:1-17), making some startling discoveries! We round out the week focusing on what God did in the events we have read up to this point, speaking a word to those who do not always find joy in the season.

In the third week, we look at the experience of Joseph, and the names he gives to his adoptive son (Matthew

---

* Many thanks to my colleague Doug Hills, who selected and edited excerpts from my sermons for this reader and then chose the prayers to go with each day's reading.

1:18-25). We also listen to the angels and shepherds as we focus on the actual birth of Jesus (Luke 2:1-21).

In the fourth week, we spend time with Simeon, the elderly saint who got to hold the infant Jesus in his arms (Luke 2:22-52). We also walk with the Magi as they journey to find the newborn King (Matthew 2:1-13). I then conclude with my attempt to summarize the message of the story for our time.

"It's the most wonderful time of year," because we once again get to live in the most wonderful story ever told.

Week 1

Readings

Now in the sixth month the angel Gabriel was sent from God to a city in Galilee called Nazareth, to a virgin engaged to a man whose name was Joseph, of the descendants of David; and the virgin's name was Mary. And coming in, he said to her, "Greetings, favored one! The Lord is with you." But she was very perplexed at this statement, and kept pondering what kind of salutation this was. The angel said to her, "Do not be afraid, Mary; for you have found favor with God. And behold, you will conceive in your womb and bear a son, and you shall name Him Jesus. He will be great and will be called the Son of the Most High; and the Lord God will give Him the throne of His father David; and He will reign over the house of Jacob forever, and His kingdom will have no end." Mary said to the angel, "How can this be, since I am a virgin?" The angel answered and said to her, "The Holy Spirit will come upon you, and the power of the Most High will overshadow you; and for that reason the holy Child shall be called the Son of God. And behold, even your relative Elizabeth has also conceived a son in her old age; and she who was called barren is now in her sixth month. For nothing will be impossible with God." And Mary said, "Behold, the bondslave of the Lord; may it be done to me according to your word." And the angel departed from her.

Now at this time Mary arose and went in a hurry to the hill country, to a city of Judah, and entered the house of Zacharias and greeted Elizabeth. When Elizabeth heard Mary's greeting, the baby leaped in her womb; and Elizabeth was filled with the Holy Spirit. And she cried out with a loud voice and said, "Blessed are you among women, and blessed is the fruit of your womb! And how has it happened to me, that the mother of my Lord would come to me? For behold, when the sound of your greeting reached my ears, the baby leaped in my womb for joy. And blessed is she who believed that there would be a fulfillment of what had been spoken to her by the Lord."

And Mary said:

> "My soul exalts the Lord, And my spirit has rejoiced in God my Savior.
> For He has had regard for the humble state of His bondslave;
> For behold, from this time on all generations will count me blessed.
> For the Mighty One has done great things for me; And holy is His name.
> And His mercy is upon generation after generation

Toward those who fear Him.
He has done mighty deeds with His arm;
He has scattered those who were proud in the
thoughts of their heart.
He has brought down rulers from their thrones,
And has exalted those who were humble.
He has filled the hungry with good things;
And sent away the rich empty-handed.
He has given help to Israel His servant,
In remembrance of His mercy,
As He spoke to our fathers,
To Abraham and his descendants forever."

And Mary stayed with her about three months, and
then returned to her home.

Luke 1:26-56

Sunday

As the story unfolds, the spotlight keeps shining on the infant Jesus. In scene after scene – in the womb in Nazareth, in the manger in Bethlehem, in the Temple in Jerusalem – the spotlight consistently shines on Jesus. He is, after all, what the story is all about. He is what the waiting of Advent and the celebration at Christmas are all about. He is, as they say, "the reason for the season."

So the spotlight keeps shining on Jesus. But as it does it also shines on the Virgin, on Mary – in the temple in Jerusalem, at the manger in Bethlehem, and in the womb in Nazareth, especially in the womb in Nazareth. Next to Jesus, Mary is the most significant person in the unfolding drama. Rightly does she sing, in her song we call "the Magnificat," "For behold, from this time on all generations will count me blessed" (Luke 1:48). Blessed indeed! Although some believers might take her blessedness to inappropriate extremes, Mary nevertheless is to be highly honoured for at least three biblical reasons.

First, Mary is the mother of our Lord. No one else has had, or can have, that privilege. You and I can be our

Lord's disciples, his apprentices. We can even be His sisters or brothers, and His Bride! But only she can be His mother. For nine months she carried Him in her womb. For years she carried Him in her arms and in her heart. It was she who nursed Him in infancy. It was she who got up at night when He cried. It was she who changed his diapers. It was she who washed His clothes, and probably even made His clothes. It was she who was there to catch Him as He first tried to walk. It was she who put Band-aids – or the first-century equivalent – on His first cuts. It was she who taught Him to speak! It was she who taught Him to pray the Psalms. It was she who gave Him his facial features: Mary is the only human being who literally bears the image of Jesus Christ. Jesus has her nose, her cheekbones, and her eyes. Mary's cousin Elizabeth, deeply moved in Mary's presence, rightly called out: "How has it happened to me, that the mother of my Lord would come to me?" (Luke 1:43).

The second reason she is to be honoured: Mary is the first Christian theologian. She is the first human being to reflect theologically on the consequences of her Son's birth. She is the first believer to articulate what the Incarnation, the enfleshment of God in our humanity, means for the world. This she does in the song she sings at Elizabeth's home, her Magnificat, her "my soul magnifies the Lord." I call her song "the Gospel according to the Virgin."

And the third reason she is to be honoured: she is the model of saving faith, the prototypical believer. I agree with biblical scholars across the theological spectrum who argue that Luke, the writer of the story, holds Mary before us as the model disciple.

"Do you want to know," Luke is asking, "what it means to believe in the miracle that is Advent-Christmas, what it means to believe in the grand miracle of the Incarnation? Do you want to know what it means to live the miracle of Christmas? Do you want to know what it means to be a disciple of the One born at Christmas? Look at Peter, and at John, and at Mary Magdalene, and at Zaccheus, and at the Apostle Paul. And look at Mary, the mother of Jesus – especially look at Mary!" Again, Elizabeth rightly honours Mary: "Blessed is she who believed that there would be a fulfillment of what had been spoken to her by the Lord" (Luke 1:45).

Mary, the mother of our Lord, is the model disciple of our Lord. She is the model disciple because she believes the impossible could happen. That is what the text emphasizes and therefore what I want to emphasize today. Mary dared to believe that the Living God could do what had never been done before, and she invites us to do the same.

Prayer

Heavenly Father,
who chose the Virgin Mary, full of grace,
to be the mother of our Lord and Saviour,
now fill us with Your grace,
that we in all things may embrace Your will
and with her rejoice in Your salvation;
through Jesus Christ our Lord,
who lives and reigns with You and the Holy Spirit,
one God, now and for ever. Amen.*

* *The Book of Alternative Services of the Anglican Church of Canada* (Toronto: Anglican Book Centre, 1985), 272.

Week 1

Monday

Although you and I will never experience what Mary did, her experience is a picture, an analogy, of what God wants to do in each of us and in human society as a whole. For nearly two thousand years, the church has "recognised that Mary's experience, which is in one way absolutely unique, in another is typical of the experience of every Christian believer."*

Growing and developing and forming in the womb of Mary is the body of the Incarnate God, Immanuel, God-with-us. That is a never-to-be repeated event! But the life, the *zoe*, the unique ungenerated, eternal life dwelling in the body growing in Mary's womb, now dwells in anyone who belongs to Mary's Son. The Living God, the God of Mary, wants to put within each of our broken lives the very life of His Son. Jesus would later say: "Abide in Me, and I in you. . . . he who abides in Me and I in him, he bears much fruit" (John 15:4-5). In you, in Me!

---

* John R. W. Stott, *The Canticles and Selected Psalms* (London: Hodder and Stoughton, 1966), 44.

The God of Advent and Christmas says to me and to you: "I will come to you in My Son, to live in you through My Spirit. And My Spirit will move in you, regenerating you, cleansing you, filling you, breaking the grip of crippling habits, overcoming the power of sin." You will begin to take on the character traits of Jesus, manifesting His love, joy, and peace. You will start to exercise Jesus' patience, kindness, and generosity. You will begin to live His faithfulness, gentleness, and self-control, and learn to deal with stress as Jesus deals with stress. You will learn to love the unloving as Jesus loves the unloving. You will learn to face death as Jesus faces death.

Like Mary we ask how – how can this be? How can this be, since I am by nature and will resistant and stubborn? How can this be, since I am so powerless over the things that seek to enslave me? How can this be, since all my life I have tried to change patterns of behaviour and not succeeded? O Lord, how can this be, since the circumstances around me seem to fight against a vital spirituality? How? The how of the miracle is a Who! The angel speaks the same message to us that He spoke to Mary: "Nothing will be impossible with God." The God of Advent and Christmas is the God of the impossible. We can be changed; the world can be changed.

And this is where Mary the model disciple comes in, for she is the model of what it means to participate in the humanly impossible. In his book *True Spirituality*, Francis

Schaeffer pointed out that Mary had three choices in the face of the humanly impossible promise, and they are the same choices that you and I face.*

First, Mary could have said: "It is impossible, period. There is no way it can happen, and I want nothing to do with it." Mary could have chosen to walk away from it all, which, sadly, is the choice many make when met by Jesus and his claims. Many say, "It is impossible," and walk away. If you are feeling that way, I urge you to reconsider. Mary did not walk away.

There is a second choice. Mary could have said: "Now that I have the promise of a child, I will exert all my effort and I myself will bring forth the Son of God." But, on her own, she could have never conceived and given birth to a Saviour. Never! So too with us. Try as we might, we cannot produce the life of Jesus in us. Though we try with all our strength, we cannot redeem ourselves. We cannot even make ourselves look redeemed! On our own we are spiritually barren and impotent. How absurd for Mary to think that she could conceive the Saviour with only human resources. How equally absurd for us to think that we can conceive, give birth to, and nurture the Saviour-life on our own. We cannot make it happen, yet we keep trying and keep getting frustrated and exhausted.

* Francis A. Schaeffer, *True Spirituality* (Wheaton, IL: Tyndale House, 1971), 57-59.

There is a third choice. It is the one Mary exercised: "Behold, the bondslave of the Lord; may it be done to me according to your word" (Luke 1:38). Mary took God at God's word. She did not completely understand it, and she did not know all that would happen. She simply admitted her inadequacy, and trusted her life to God's promise. Or, as I should say, she trusted her life to the God Who promises. In the face of human impossibility, she opens herself up to the One Who is bigger than humanity, and says, "Here I am Lord. I cannot make this happen. But you can. I give myself to you . . . fulfill Your Word in me."

Prayer

Visiting God,
eclipse my doubts and questions
with the brightness of Your presence,
and, like Mary, overshadow my life with Your Holy Spirit
conceiving in me a true faith that receives Jesus Christ,
making him my own and me Your favored one. Amen.[*]

---

[*] Philip F. Reinders, *Seeking God's Face: Praying with the Bible through the Year* (Grand Rapids: Faith Alive Christian Resources, 2012), 67.

Tuesday

The Virgin Mary is the first Christian theologian. Mary is the first human being to reflect theologically and biblically on the meaning of the birth of Jesus. Mary is the first person to try to put into words what the miracle and mystery of the Incarnation means for the world.

Mary does her theological and biblical reflection on what is happening for the world in the conception and birth of her Child through song. She is carrying in her womb the Saviour of the world! And she sings what it all means for her, for Israel, and for the world.

Today, let us focus on the most arresting Gospel truth Mary sings: what God is doing in her and in the world is all accomplished by the arm of the Lord. "He has done mighty deeds with His arm" (Luke 1:51). Arm, a little word, but like a lot of little words in the Bible, a big truth. Mary knows of the great story, so she knows where the phrase "the arm of the Lord" comes into play. At the Exodus, at the liberation from Egypt, God says, "I will also redeem you with an outstretched arm" (Exodus 6:6). After the Exile, at the liberation from Babylon, Scripture says:

"Like a shepherd He will tend His flock, in His arm He will gather the lambs, and carry them in His bosom" (Isaiah 40:11).

And the phrase echoes through the greatest poetic section of the Old Testament, Isaiah 51-53. I think Mary loved this section of the Bible, and I think she taught it to her Son. "Awake, awake, put on strength, O arm of the Lord" (Isaiah 51:9). "How lovely on the mountains are the feet of him who brings good news, who announces peace and brings good news of happiness, who announces salvation, and says to Zion, 'Your God reigns!'" (Isaiah 52:7).

In her Son, Mary sees God living out what the poetry of Isaiah says about God's arm. That is, she sees in the coming of her Son, God stretching out His arm. Mary realizes a great reversal of values will take place because she realizes that the great reversal is rooted in an even greater reversal – in the reversal of all the imagery we would naturally associate with the arm of God. Listen to Isaiah 52:10: "The Lord has bared His holy arm." Yeah! The expectation is that God does so in all the ways we humans think about when we think of might and power: "Go get 'em God!"

But Mary knows her Bible. She knows how the poetry continues: "To whom has the arm of the Lord been revealed?" (Isaiah 53:1). And we read on: "For He grew up before Him like a tender shoot, and like a root out of parched ground; He has no stately form or majesty that we should look upon Him" (Isaiah 53:2). "To whom has the arm of the Lord been revealed?" "He was despised and forsaken of men, a man of sorrows and acquainted with grief" (Isaiah 53:3). "Surely our griefs He Himself bore, and our sorrows He carried . . . . He was pierced through for our transgressions, He was crushed for our iniquities; the chastening for our well-being fell upon Him, and by His scourging we are healed" (Isaiah 53:4-5).

Isaiah, the greatest Old Testament theologian, sees that the arm of the Lord turns out to be the suffering servant of the Lord. And Mary, the first New Testament theologian, sees in Jesus that servant-arm. I know she sees this because in verse 54 of her song she refers to Israel the servant. The only place in the Bible where Israel is called "servant" is in the poetic songs of Isaiah, in the so-called "Servant Songs."

Do you see where this is going? Mary sees in her Child the arm of the Lord. God is now going to bare His arm. And is going to do so in a surprising way! God is going to bare His arm on a Roman cross. God flexes His muscles by hanging on a cross. The out-stretched arms of Jesus are the out-stretched arms of God. "The Lord has bared His holy arm." He exalts Himself to show mercy. God wins His victory over sin and evil and death by letting sin and evil and death win over Him. God wins His victory through weaknesses and vulnerability. God's arm accomplishes His mightiest work in the moment when He is least competent, when His arm is immobilized by nails binding Him to a cross! I am not saying Mary saw all this while Jesus was still in her womb. But I am saying that she knew, if only for a moment, where her son would have to go. "The Lord has bared His arm": "By oppression and judgment He was taken away; . . . He was cut off out of the land of the living for the transgression of My people, to whom the stroke was due" (Isaiah 53:8).

Prayer

Son of David,
today I bow before You as my true King.
You subdue me by humbling Yourself as a helpless baby,
You rule me by subjecting Yourself,
You defend me through a chubby infant's arm,
and the hand of power that conquers all enemies
is curled around a mother's finger.
Amen.

Wednesday

The reason we have not heard more preaching on Mary's Magnificat is that the church has not known how to handle it, especially the middle section, Luke 1:51-53. What are we to do with this part of the Advent-Christmas story?

He has scattered those who were proud in the thoughts of their heart. He has brought down rulers from their thrones, and has exalted those who were humble. He has filled the hungry with good things, and sent away the rich empty-handed.

Have you ever seen those words printed on a Hallmark Christmas card? The Good News Translation renders Mary's words even more boldly:

[He has] scattered the proud with all their plans. He has brought down mighty kings from their thrones, and lifted up the lowly. He has filled the hungry with good things and sent the rich away with empty hands.

It would be hard to find any more revolutionary words!

Under the inspiration of the Holy Spirit, Mary sees God's choice of her as the beginning of a great reversal.

Who was she to be chosen as the mother of the world's Saviour? Who was she, a woman of " low estate" as she puts it in her song, to be chosen to be mother of the King of kings and Lord of lords? Yet, God chose her! And she comes to realize that God's choice of her is a particular instance of a larger pattern. New Testament scholar George Caird observes that "Mary sings of her own exaltation from lowliness to greatness as typical of the new order which is to open out for the whole people of God through the coming of her son."* Mary realizes, if only for a moment, that when her Son is born into our world, a great reversal begins, and a great revolution starts.

Now, Mary herself is no revolutionary. Nazareth is not the secret headquarters for a violent wing of the Zealot party. She is one of the pious folks who had long ago given up hope in any human ideology, system, or leader to bring about the kingdom of heaven on earth. Mary is not a social or political agitator. It is just that, under the inspiration of the Holy Spirit, she comes to understand that her Son, who when He became an adult was no revolutionary either, will effect radical reversal in every sector of human life.

Mary sees in her particular case three specific instances of what is typical of her Son's new order. In the coming

* G. B. Caird, *Saint Luke* (Philadelphia: Westminster Press, 1963), 55.

of Jesus of Nazareth, God shows mercy to those who fear Him, and scatters those who are proud in the thoughts of their hearts. In his coming, God exalts the humble, and brings down the mighty from the thrones. And, God fills the hungry with good things, and sends the rich away empty handed.

Notice that Mary puts all of this in the past tense: has scattered, has exalted, has brought down, has filled, has sent away. Jesus is not yet born – He is still in her womb – yet she uses past tense verbs. Why? Because in her particular case, the old order of things has already been set aside and overturned. In her particular case, the proud, mighty, and rich have been passed over; in her particular case, God has already lifted up those who fear Him, who are humble, and who are hungry. But she uses the past tense verb for other reasons: "With sudden insight she realizes what the end of it all will be, and rejoices that since God has set his saving work in motion, it is already as good as done."*

Mary's song is not a call to revolution, for Mary is not celebrating human achievement. She is not singing about work done by human beings, proud or humble, rich or poor. The key word in her Magnificat is a pronoun: He. He has shown mercy. He has brought down. He has lifted

---

* Michael Wilcock, *The Savior of the World: The Message of Luke's Gospel* (Downers Grove, IL: InterVarsity, 1979), 36.

up. He has sent away. He has done great things. He turns the world upside down. And when He does, I want to be found on his side.

Prayer

Life-giving God,
we thank You for calling Mary to be the mother of Jesus.
In a world where men were in control,
You chose a young girl to nurture the Saviour of the world.
In a world where power is sought, You
turned our values upside-down
by inviting Mary to share in the great work of redemption.
We thank you that still you call women and
men to share in Your saving actions.
Help us to say 'Yes' when You call.
Enlarge our vision, strengthen our resolve,
and increase our sense of Your all-sufficient grace,
that we might be used mightily for Your
glory and for the serving of Your world;
through Jesus Christ our Lord. Amen.[*]

* Adapted from *Gathering for Worship: Patterns and Prayers for the Community of Disciples* (Norwich: Canterbury Press, 2005), 356.

Thursday

Throughout most of church history, Christians have tended to spiritualize Mary's song. That is, we have tended to apply her words and images to the personal, private realm of life. And to a certain degree, this is appropriate. None of us enters the fullness of salvation until we confess our pride and learn what it means to fear God. Jesus Christ is formed in us as we recognize how far short we have fallen from the glory of God, and then admit our need for a Saviour. Furthermore, none of us comes into the fullness of salvation until we humble ourselves and come off the throne of our life. Jesus Christ is formed in us as we surrender the reins and submit to His lordship. None of us comes into the fullness of salvation until we acknowledge our spiritual poverty and long for the true riches of God's Spirit. Jesus Christ is formed in us as we come to him empty handed, seeking what only He can give. So to a degree, it is appropriate to spiritualize Mary's revolutionary song. But, in so doing, we miss the wider scope of the salvation that the Magnificat celebrates.

"My soul exalts the Lord, and my spirit has rejoiced in God my Savior . . . His mercy is upon generation after generation toward those who fear Him. . . . He has scattered those who were proud in the thoughts of their heart" (Luke 1:46-51). The coming of Jesus causes ideological reversals, reversals in our presuppositions about life and God's ways in the world. We confront this reversal right from the beginning of Jesus' life in the world. Nothing fits the normal paradigms! Here is Immanuel, God the Creator comes to earth. And where does He choose to touch down? In Bethlehem, in a small barrio, lost in the shadow of Jerusalem. If we had planned his coming, we would have picked a more strategic place like Rome. Imagine a big gala celebration in the Coliseum complete with cheerleaders and media coverage. Or Athens, with all the philosophers seated in the Parthenon. Or at least in Jerusalem, on the steps of the magnificent temple Herod built. But God chose Bethlehem, a spot off the beaten path, far from where the media says the action is.

Even if we had chosen Bethlehem, we would have at least had Mary and Joseph ride into town in a chariot or a horse-drawn cart. But no, here they come on a donkey. And would we not have picked a girl from a more established family, someone who understood royalty and power – a daughter of Caesar Augustus, for example? As far as the rest of the world was concerned, Mary and her kind were the nobodies of the world. And the way God came through Mary, through her virgin's womb – without male sperm conjoining with female ovum. It does not fit the paradigm. It does not square with our presuppositions about what can or cannot happen. Often on Christmas Eve, as I reflect on the way He came, I think I can hear God saying what He said long ago through the Prophet Isaiah: "My thoughts are not your thoughts, nor are your ways my ways" (Isaiah 55:8).

Is this not the case with the new thing God is doing in his Church around the world? It is not fitting the Christendom paradigm, the nineteenth and twentieth century paradigm. It is fitting the Biblical model, but not the model of the church under Christendom. "My ways are not your ways."

And is this not the case in our personal lives? How many times do we cry out for mercy and God answers . . . but not in ways we imagine He would. Why do God's acts of mercy keep catching us by surprise? Could it be that, after all, we really do not fear God? Could it be that we do not regularly stand in awe of God? Could it be that we simply do not take God seriously enough? That we do not take the Presence and Power of God in the drama of history seriously enough? We do not take Jesus seriously enough when He announces His Gospel. We do not take seriously Jesus' teaching about how the kingdom comes into the world. Could it be that we are "proud in the thoughts of our hearts," as Mary puts it, that we think we know how to make it all work? Or we expect God to do it according to our paradigms? Mary realizes that only those who fear God, who honour God as God, actually live in the new work of God in the world.

Prayer

God, You have made Yourself known,
but in a most amazing way,
coming in weakness, in a tiny baby;
You covered Your glory and hid Your greatness.
God of mystery and surprise, we praise You.
God, You have made Yourself known,
but in a most amazing way,
in a dirty poor stable no one else wanted;
You hid Your wealth and infinite riches.
God of mystery and surprise, we praise You.
God, You have made Yourself known,
but in a most amazing way,
born to humble working people, hidden in a simple life,
and yet announced in the stars of
heaven and visited by kings.
God of mystery and surprise, we praise You. Amen.*

---

* *The Worship Sourcebook* (Grand Rapids: Faith Alive, 2004), 497-98.

Week 1

Friday

"My soul exalts the Lord, and my spirit has rejoiced in God my Savior ... He has brought down rulers from their thrones, and has exalted those who were humble" (Luke 1:46, 52). The word "humble" or "lowly" refers to those who have no access to the power structures of a society. To those who must therefore throw themselves on God for vindication and deliverance. The coming of Jesus causes social status reversals. The mighty are brought down, and the humble are exalted. Again, Mary is not a radical liberation theologian, but under the inspiration of the Holy Spirit she sees the consequences of the birth of her Son.

"Mighty brought down ... humble exalted." Matthew tells us that when the magi from the east came to Jerusalem looking for the new-born king, King Herod was "greatly troubled" (Matthew 2:3). Herod senses that the birth of King Jesus has massive implications for his government, and he is deeply troubled. So were the scribes and chief priests. Did they need to be? That is the question: Do they need to feel troubled?

This note of God bringing down and raising up is sounded throughout the Bible. In the prophet Daniel, for instance, we read about Nebuchadnezzar, King of Babylon. In chapter four we are told that Nebuchadnezzar suffered a recurring nightmare. He kept seeing a huge tree, strong and fruitful, being chopped down. And he kept seeing a man taking on animal-like characteristics, tormented in mind and soul. Daniel is called upon to interpret the dream. He tells the king that the tree being chopped down means his government is being taken away, "until you recognize that the Most High is ruler over the realm of humankind, and bestows it on whomever He wishes" (Daniel 4:25).

The man taking on animal-like characteristics means that Nebuchadnezzar was to be driven into exile among the beasts until he came to his senses and recognized that "heaven rules." And Daniel tells the king that the proof he has come to his senses is that he does justice, turns from immorality, and shows mercy to the poor. Nebuchadnezzar did finally wake up to true reality, humbled himself before the Living God, and saw his kingdom restored.

Mary knows the secret most rulers on their thrones do not. God brings down rulers who ignore God's rule and exalts those who seek God's rule – it is only a matter of when and how. If Herod will not change his ways, he has very good reason to be frightened by the news of the birth of the new King. Mary means what she sings.

Now, as I have tried to listen to the Magnificat on its own terms, the question has emerged: "Do the mighty have to come down in order for the humble to be exalted?" The conclusion I have reached is "not necessarily." The mighty can choose to humble themselves before the Almighty and give themselves in service to the Almighty by lifting up the humble. That is the message of many portions of Scripture, especially Psalm 72, where we find the portfolio of the rulers who please God and receive God's blessing. Listen to a few lines:

> Give the king your judgments, O God,
> And Your righteousness to the king's son!
> May he judge Your people with righteousness
> And your afflicted with justice!
> Let the mountains bring peace to the people,
> And the hills in righteousness.
> May he vindicate the afflicted of the people,
> Save the children of the needy,
> And crush the oppressor.
> Let them fear You while the sun endures,
> And as long as the moon, throughout all generations.
> . . .
> For he will deliver the needy when he cries for help,
> The afflicted also, and him who has no helper.
> He will have compassion on the poor and needy,
> And the lives of the needy he will save.

> Psalm 72:1-5, 12-13

Prayer

O Lord, our God,
as we celebrate again the festival of Christmas,
we ask You to make us humble and loving like Jesus,
who did not come to be served but to serve,
and who said that it is better to give than to receive,
so that in His name
we may devote ourselves to the care
and service of all who are in need.
We ask this through the same Jesus
Christ, our Lord. Amen.[*]

* *The Worship Sourcebook* (Grand Rapids: Faith Alive, 2004), 473.

Week 1

Saturday

My soul exalts the Lord, and my spirit has rejoiced in God my Savior . . . He has filled the hungry with good things, and sent away the rich empty-handed" (Luke 1:46, 53). The coming of Jesus causes economic reversals. Mary sings for joy because in her Son a new order of economic justice is breaking into the world. It is this part of the Virgin's Song that makes many of us uneasy – for many of us are the rich of the world, whose hands are filled with good things.

Now, as I have tried to listen to the Magnificat on its own terms, a question emerges: "Must the rich be sent away empty-handed in order to fill the hungry with good things?" Is that what Mary is saying? Some Christians answer "yes" and then voluntarily let go of all the good things in their hands. Some conclude that in order to be faithful to Jesus' claim on their lives, they must sell everything, give the proceeds to the poor, and become one with the poor. Saint Francis of Assisi is the most shining example of this. He considered himself "married to poverty." Some of you may wrestle with a similar pull in your soul.

Must all rich disciples of Mary's Son, the Son of God, go that way in order for the hungry to be filled with good things? Is that what Mary is singing? No, but if her Son is being formed in us, there will be a growing sensitivity to the plight of the hungry. There will be a growing desire to fill the hungry, especially to see the hungry filled with Jesus Himself, the Bread of Life. It is inevitable, for that is Jesus' desire. And if He is formed in me, I will be alive in His desire.

Luke will draw this out in the rest of his Gospel. I think of the story of Zaccheus the tax-collector. Jesus had dinner in Zaccheus' house and after dinner said, "Today salvation has come to this house" (Luke 19:9). What was the sign that salvation has come? "Lord," said Zaccheus, "half of my possessions I will give to the poor, and if I have defrauded anyone of anything, I will give back four times as much" (Luke 19:8). Who told Zaccheus to do that? No one! The encounter with Mary's Son broke the power of greed and empowered Zaccheus to renounce unethical business practices. His encounter with Jesus set him free to open his hands in outrageous generosity.

Salvation, the kind wrought in Mary's Son, the Son of God, impacts economies, finances, bank accounts, and VISA cards. Jesus Christ being formed within us changes our relationships to "the good things" in our hands. We realize that we really do not own these good things and never really have. They are all His; indeed, all things are

His. We are stewards of His things, and we realize the one thing required of stewards is that they be faithful to the master's desires. This will manifest itself in a growing desire to simplify our life styles, to be unencumbered by the demands that all those good things place on us. He comes to set the captives free! It will manifest itself in dreaming of creative ways to put our possessions and wealth to use for the kingdom of God.

And as Mary's Son is formed in us, there will be a growing desire to become advocates for the powerless. It is inevitable, for Jesus Himself is their greatest advocate. We begin to realize that charity, as good as it is, is not good enough. We can give and give and give and never effect any real change. For we soon discover that the problem lives in systems that keep the hungry hungry. What is needed is not only charity, but also advocacy, voices in the systems who speak for the voiceless, voices who embrace the Virgin's vision of Her Son. "Is not that what it means to know Me," the Lord asks through Jeremiah, to plead "the cause of the afflicted and needy?" (Jeremiah 22:16).

Prayer

Lord Jesus Christ,

our deliverer,

Your birth still shakes the foundations of our world.

May we wait for Your return

with such eagerness and hope

that we embrace without terror

the labor pangs of Your coming kingdom. Amen.[*]

---

[*] *The Worship Sourcebook* (Grand Rapids: Faith Alive, 2004), 430.

WEEK 2

Readings

Inasmuch as many have undertaken to compile an account of the things accomplished among us, just as they were handed down to us by those who from the beginning were eyewitnesses and servants of the word, it seemed fitting for me as well, having investigated everything carefully from the beginning, to write it out for you in consecutive order, most excellent Theophilus; so that you may know the exact truth about the things you have been taught.

In the days of Herod, king of Judea, there was a priest named Zacharias, of the division of Abijah; and he had a wife from the daughters of Aaron, and her name was Elizabeth. They were both righteous in the sight of God, walking blamelessly in all the commandments and requirements of the Lord. But they had no child, because Elizabeth was barren, and they were both advanced in years.

Now it happened that while he was performing his priestly service before God in the appointed order of his division, according to the custom of the priestly office, he was chosen by lot to enter the temple of the Lord and burn incense. And the whole multitude of the people were in prayer outside at the hour of the incense offering. And an angel of the Lord appeared to him, standing to the right of the altar of incense. Zacharias was troubled when he saw the angel, and fear gripped him. But the angel said to him, "Do not be afraid, Zacharias, for your petition has been heard, and your wife Elizabeth will bear you a son, and you will give him the name John. You will have joy and gladness, and many will rejoice at his birth. For he will be great in the sight of the Lord; and he will drink no wine or liquor, and he will be filled with the Holy Spirit while yet in his mother's womb. And he will turn many of the sons of Israel back to the Lord their God. It is he who will go as a forerunner before Him in the spirit and power of Elijah, to turn the hearts of the fathers back to the children, and the disobedient to the attitude of the righteous, so as to make ready a people prepared for the Lord."

Zacharias said to the angel, "How will I know this for certain? For I am an old man and my wife is advanced in years." The angel answered and said to him, "I am Gabriel, who stands in the presence of God, and I have been sent to speak to you and to bring you this good news. And behold, you shall be silent and unable to speak until the day when these things take place, because you did not believe my words, which will be fulfilled in their proper time."

The people were waiting for Zacharias, and were wondering at his delay in the temple. But when he came out, he was unable to speak to them; and they realized that he had seen a vision in the temple; and he kept making signs to them, and remained mute. When the days of his priestly service were ended, he went back home.

Luke 1:1-25

Now the time had come for Elizabeth to give birth, and she gave birth to a son. Her neighbors and her relatives heard that the Lord had displayed His great mercy toward her; and they were rejoicing with her.

And it happened that on the eighth day they came to circumcise the child, and they were going to call him Zacharias, after his father. But his mother answered and said, "No indeed; but he shall be called John." And they said to her, "There is no one among your relatives who is called by that name." And they made signs to his father, as to what he wanted him called. And he asked for a tablet and wrote as follows, "His name is John." And they were all astonished. And at once his mouth was opened and his tongue loosed, and he began to speak in praise of God. Fear came on all those living around them; and all these matters were being talked about in all the hill country of Judea. All who heard them kept them in mind, saying, "What then will this child turn out to be?" For the hand of the Lord was certainly with him.

And his father Zacharias was filled with the Holy Spirit, and prophesied, saying:

"Blessed be the Lord God of Israel,
For He has visited us and accomplished redemption for His people,
And has raised up a horn of salvation for us
In the house of David His servant –
As He spoke by the mouth of His holy prophets from of old –
Salvation from our enemies,
And from the hand of all who hate us;
To show mercy toward our fathers,
And to remember His holy covenant,
The oath which He swore to Abraham our father,
To grant us that we, being rescued from the hand of our enemies,
Might serve Him without fear,
In holiness and righteousness before Him all our days.
"And you, child, will be called the prophet of the Most High;
For you will go on before the Lord to prepare His ways;
To give to His people the knowledge of salvation
By the forgiveness of their sins,
Because of the tender mercy of our God,

With which the Sunrise from on high will visit us,
To shine upon those who sit in darkness and the
shadow of death,
To guide our feet into the way of peace."

And the child continued to grow and to become strong in spirit, and he lived in the deserts until the day of his public appearance to Israel.

Luke 1:57-80

The record of the genealogy of Jesus the Messiah, the son of David, the son of Abraham:

Abraham was the father of Isaac, Isaac the father of Jacob, and Jacob the father of Judah and his brothers. Judah was the father of Perez and Zerah by Tamar, Perez was the father of Hezron, and Hezron the father of Ram. Ram was the father of Amminadab, Amminadab the father of Nahshon, and Nahshon the father of Salmon. Salmon was the father of Boaz by Rahab, Boaz was the father of Obed by Ruth, and Obed the father of Jesse. Jesse was the father of David the king.

David was the father of Solomon by Bathsheba who had been the wife of Uriah. Solomon was the father of Rehoboam, Rehoboam the father of Abijah, and Abijah the father of Asa. Asa was the father of Jehoshaphat, Jehoshaphat the father of Joram, and Joram the father of Uzziah. Uzziah was the father of Jotham, Jotham the father of Ahaz, and Ahaz the father of Hezekiah. Hezekiah was the father of Manasseh, Manasseh the father of Amon, and Amon the father of Josiah. Josiah became the father of Jeconiah and his brothers, at the time of the deportation to Babylon.

After the deportation to Babylon: Jeconiah became the father of Shealtiel, and Shealtiel the father of Zerubbabel. Zerubbabel was the father of Abihud, Abihud the father of Eliakim, and Eliakim the father of Azor. Azor was the father of Zadok, Zadok the father of Achim, and Achim the father of Eliud. Eliud was the father of Eleazar, Eleazar the father of Matthan, and Matthan the father of Jacob. Jacob was the father of Joseph the husband of Mary, by whom Jesus was born, who is called the Messiah.

So all the generations from Abraham to David are fourteen generations; from David to the deportation to Babylon, fourteen generations; and from the deportation to Babylon to the Messiah, fourteen generations.

Matthew 1:1-17

Week 2

Sunday

Zacharias and his wife Elizabeth loved God with all their heart (Luke 1:6-7). Such love, however, did not insulate them against the pains of life in a broken world. All their married life they had wanted children, but they were unable to make it happen. Each passing month and year deepened the pain. Then one day, as Zacharias, who was a priest, was praying in the temple, an angelic messenger brought him tremendous news: "Do not be afraid, Zacharias, for your petition has been heard, and your wife Elizabeth will bear you a son, and you will give him the name John" (Luke 1:13). And then the angel went on to tell him about who his son would be (Luke 1:14-17).

To say the least, Zacharias was startled by this encounter and message. In fact, he found it all hard to believe: "How will I know this for certain? For I am an old man and my wife is advanced in years" (Luke 1:18). Zacharias, understandably, needed some tangible sign of the validity of this promise.

God responded, and made Zacharias unable to speak until the day the child would be born (Luke 1:19-20).

He got more than he bargained for – nine months of no speaking! Finally the day came, and Elizabeth delivered a son; when the boy was eight days old, the extended family gathered together to circumcise and name him. And Zacharias was filled with the Holy Spirit, his mouth was opened, his tongue was loosed, and his heart burst forth in praise, singing his powerful "Benedictus." Oh, how he sang!

His song is not just the boasting of a proud father. Yes, Zacharias rejoices in the role John is given: he is to be the forerunner, the one who prepares the way for the Lord. But Zacharias's song is not primarily about his son, John. Indeed, by the end of the song, his son is outshone by a great Son (Luke 1:78). Zacharias's spirit soars in praise because he sees, in the One who comes after his son, the coming of God!

Zacharias's great insight is that his son will announce the advent of God! "Blessed be the Lord God of Israel, for He has visited us" (Luke 1:68). Zacharias realizes that Christmas is all about God's visitation of the world.

"God has visited us!" That is what causes Zacharias to sing for joy. In the birth of his son, the living God has begun a process whereby God is entering history in Person. This is not to say that God has been absent from history up to this point – quite the contrary. But Zacharias came to realize that the birth of his son was the prelude to a totally unique event, a history-dividing event – the Living God visiting the world in person.

Two words capture God's motivation for visitation. The first is faithfulness. God had made specific promises to specific persons of the past. Zacharias refers to the prophets, to the ancestors, to David, and to Abraham. Zacharias sees, in the birth of his son and Mary's Son, God's fulfillment of those covenants. Christmas declares the faithfulness of the Promise-Maker: God did what God said he would do. This great truth is affirmed in the Hebrew names for those involved in the Christmas Story – Zacharias means "God has remembered," and Elizabeth means "God is oath" or "God is the absolutely faithful one."[*]

There is an even deeper motive for God's visitation. Driving God's faithfulness is God's mercy. Twice Zacharias sings of it: God has visited us "to show mercy toward our fathers" (Luke 1:72), and "because of the tender mercy of our God, with which the Sunrise from on high will visit us" (Luke 1:78).

The God of Christmas is not the God of the philosophers, the unmoved mover, lost in lofty contemplation of the Divine self. The God of Christmas is the passionate God, who sympathizes and empathizes, who feels our hurts and longings and fears. The God of Christmas is full

[*] John R. W. Stott, *Canticles and Psalms* (London: Hodder and Stoughton, 1966), 38.

of tender mercy. Again, this truth is affirmed in a Hebrew name for one of the characters in the Christmas Story, for John means "God is merciful."

Faithfulness and mercy – that is why Christmas happens. The Living God has made covenants and is keeping them. The Living God feels for human beings in bondage and darkness and is doing something about it. What thrilled the heart of Zacharias is that Christmas is not an afterthought, but the fulfillment of promise that emerges out of the depths of Divine compassion.

Prayer
Wise God,
thank You that Christ's incarnation
was not a quick reaction to surprising circumstances
but part of Your eternal purpose,
the unfolding of Your long-ago decreed will.
To think that my salvation is part of
Your grand eternal purpose
leaves me stunned with joy-filled awe. Amen.

Week 2

Monday

As Zacharias bursts into song over the joy of God's visitation, and as he rejoices over the faithfulness and mercy of God that stand behind that visitation, he also is thrilled by the goals of God's visitation. Zacharias sings of at least four great purposes in God coming to the world personally.

First, God came to redeem: "Blessed be the Lord God of Israel, for He has visited us and accomplished redemption for His people" (Luke 1:68). The word "redeem" always refers to a situation in which someone is caught in some sort of bondage from which the person cannot free him or herself. God visits us to set us free from all that binds us! Sing, Zacharias, sing!

In the first part of his song, Zacharias seems to speak of God's redeeming work in military and political terms: "Salvation from our enemies, and from the hand of all who hate us" (Luke 1:71). For centuries, Israel understood redemption primarily in those terms: Israel would be free to be God's people if she were free of foreign domination.

But through the prophets, God made it increasingly clear that the real enemy of God's people was not foreign oppressors. What kept them from being whole persons was sin and the consequences of sin – guilt and death. Thus, in the later part of his song, Zacharias changes tunes and speaks of God coming to effect "the forgiveness of their sins" (Luke 1:77). How contrary to Israel's expectations! God is saying that their greatest need was not to be freed from other people's sin, but from their own sin. So too, us – as individuals and as a society. We need a mighty, mighty Redeemer, someone strong enough to break the yoke of sin.

But there is more – a second goal of God's visitation. Freedom *from* is not the end; there is a freedom *for*. Zacharias goes on to sing that God has visited us "to grant us that we, being rescued from the hand of our enemies, might serve Him without fear" (Luke 1:74). God comes to us as Jesus Christ to set us free *from* sin, *for* intimacy with God without fear.

Before God's merciful visitation, people felt they could only approach God in fear and trembling (see Isaiah 6:5). God's visitation would change all of that. God's coming in Person would remove the sin barrier and set people free to come to God fearlessly. Zacharias does not know that this will involve the crucifixion of his nephew, but he does know that in Jesus, God is doing all that is necessary for us to know and enjoy God without any fear.

There is still more to the goal of God's visitation. God has visited us, sings Zacharias, "to shine upon those who sit in darkness and the shadow of death" (Luke 1:79). The coming of God in Jesus is the beginning of the end of the world's long night. Zacharias expresses it in a lovely image: "The Sunrise from on high will visit us" (Luke 1:78). Because of Christmas, it is now the dawn, that pregnant moment when there is only a small glimmer of light on the horizon, but when, in an instant, in every direction, the sky begins to light up and the land becomes visible. God's visitation means the coming of light, shining into all the dark corners of our lives, not to embarrass or condemn, but to cleanse and to heal.

There is still more – a fourth goal. "Blessed be the Lord God of Israel, for He has visited us . . . to guide our feet into the way of peace" (Luke 1:79). God comes to lead us out of darkness and death into the path of peace. Oh, how we need such visitation.

In singing of peace, Zacharias is referring to more than the absence of strife, to more than the absence of war. He is referring to all that makes for life as God originally intended it. *Shalom* is the Hebrew word – it means "soundness, wholeness, well-being." Zacharias has to sing, for he realizes that God is coming to the world in Person to bring us into the very well-being that God enjoys within God's own self.

What amazes me is that Zacharias sang his song with such joy when the visitation was only in embryonic form. We have so much more to go on from this side of the birth of Jesus, and from this side of Jesus' life, death, resurrection, and ascension. All the more can we sing, and with even greater joy!

Prayer

O promised Christ:
We are a world at war.
Our peace depends on Your coming.
We are a sinful people.
Our pardon depends on Your coming.
We are full of good intentions but
weak at keeping promises;
our only hope of doing God's will
is that You should come and help us do it.
Lord Christ, Word made flesh: our world waits
for Your peace,
for Your pardon,
and for Your grace.
Even so, come, Lord Jesus. Amen.[*]

---

[*] *The Worship Sourcebook* (Grand Rapids: Faith Alive, 2004), 441.

Tuesday

I know that many of you would prefer that we skip over the genealogies given in Matthew 1:1-14. Raymond Brown, in his monumental work *The Birth of the Messiah,* writes: "To the modern reader there are few things in the Bible less meaningful than the frequent lists of descendants or ancestors."* You would most certainly not find this text printed on holiday greeting cards! What a strange, and on first reading boring, way to begin the greatest story ever told.

But to the Jewish mind it was the most natural and most significant way to begin: if you know a person's personal pedigree, you know the person. In fact, you did not know the person unless you knew his or her pedigree. This was especially the case when one was being considered for the position of priest or king (see Ezra 2:62-63; Nehe-

---

* Raymond E. Brown, *The Birth of the Messiah: A Commentary on the Infancy Narratives in Matthew and Luke* (Garden City, NY: Doubleday, 1977), 64.

miah 7:64-65). Candidates had to be able to demonstrate that they were pure Jews.

What is Matthew telling us about Jesus in the way he presents Jesus' pedigree? Clearly, Matthew is claiming that Mary's child is the Jewish Messiah, the anointed one, the Christ. And the Jewish mind would have gotten that claim right away.

But the Jewish mind would have heard Matthew making an even more startling claim in the first two words that he writes: "book . . . genesis" (1:1). That is literally how the tax-collector-turned-evangelist begins his introduction to his Advent Christmas story: "book . . . genesis . . . Jesus Christ."

Genesis. What does Matthew want us to see? The words he uses, *biblios geneseos*, are intended to take our minds back to two well-known passages of the Old Testament: Genesis 2:4 and Genesis 5:1.* In the Greek version, Genesis 2:4 reads, *Biblios geneseos* – "the book of the genesis of heaven and earth"; Genesis 5:1 reads, *Biblios geneseos* – "the book of the genesis of Adam." In both cases what is then described in "the book of the genesis of . . . " is a creative work of God, God bringing into being that which did not previously exist.

* George Beasley-Murray, *Matthew* (London: Scripture Union, 1984), 17.

Matthew is declaring in his opening words that what follows is the story of a whole new creative work of God! *Biblios geneseos.* The pedigree that follows does not simply describe a nice little Jewish boy born to a nice Jewish couple one star-filled night. The pedigree that follows describes the beginning of a second Genesis. The birth of this child inaugurates "a new era for humanity and the world."* What Matthew is declaring in his opening words is that the child is the New Creation, the New Adam, the New Humanity. "The book of the genesis of Jesus Christ."

This startling claim made at the beginning of the pedigree is sounded with greater force at the end. Listen again to how Matthew puts it: "The book of the genesis of Jesus Christ, son of David, son of Abraham. Abraham was the father of Isaac, Isaac the father of Jacob, Jacob the father of Judah, Judah the father of Perez and Zerah . . . ." And on it goes, "D the father of E, E the father of F . . . ," until we come to the end: "Eleazar the father of Matthan, Matthan the father of Jacob, Jacob the father of Joseph, the husband of Mary, of whom was born Jesus, who is called the Christ." Did you hear the break in the cadence? Not: X the father of Y, Y the father of Z, Z the father of Jesus who is called Christ. But: X the father

---

* David Hill, *The Gospel of Matthew* [New Century Bible Commentary] (Grand Rapids: Wm. B. Eerdmans, 1972), 74-75.

of Y, Y the father of Z, Z *the husband of Mary* of whom was born Jesus who is called the Christ.

The point? The Christmas Child, although very human, comes into being in an extra-ordinary way. Although he comes through humanity, he is not produced by humanity. Although Jesus Christ comes from the womb of a human being, he is not begotten by a human being. This is a new and different act of God, as new and as unique and as un-precedented as the first genesis. The child born of Mary is a brand new creative work of God!

"The book of the genesis of Jesus Christ." Mary's child is the new creation!

Prayer

Creator God,
We thank You for the gift of creation.
We rejoice that You spoke into the
darkness, sent light into our world,
and now invite us to enjoy the blessings of our world.
We confess that too often we have not treated
Your creation as the good gift that it is.
We thank You also for the gift of Your new creation.
We rejoice that You once more spoke into
the darkness, sent light into our world,
and now invite us to enjoy the blessings of Your Son.
May we this day see and accept with joy
Your creative work in our lives. Amen.

Wednesday

Matthew includes the names of four women in addition to Mary in Jesus' pedigree. Tamar, the mother of Perez and Zerah (Matthew 1:3); Rahab, the mother of Boaz (Matthew 1:5); Ruth, the mother of Obed (Matthew 1:5); and "the wife of Uriah," Bathsheba, the mother of Solomon (Matthew 1:6).

Now this is truly amazing! In the first century women's names were not ordinarily included in genealogical tables. Women had no legal rights or status. A woman was, in legal terms, simply a man's property. So what would be gained by including women in one's genealogy, in a document whose purpose is to establish a man's reputation? Why would you put a woman's name in that kind of document?

What is even more amazing about this fact is that three of these four women were foreigners, not pure Jews: Tamar was a Canaanite, Rahab a Jerichoite, Ruth a Moabite, and Bathsheba, although a Jew by birth, was technically no longer so, for through her marriage to Uriah, she became a Hittite. Here in the gene-pool of the New Creation are these Gentiles. Gentiles!

What is still more amazing is that three of the four women had done morally questionable things (to say the least!). Tamar had seduced her father-in-law Judah, and was an adulteress (see Genesis 38). Rahab was a prostitute (see Joshua 2). Bathsheba had an affair with King David (see 2 Samuel 11). And Ruth, although herself morally upright, as a Moabite was a descendent of incestuous Lot (see Genesis 19). It was said that no "Moabite shall enter the assembly of the Lord; none of their descendants, even to the tenth generation" (Deuteronomy 23:3). And yet a Moabite woman is in the pedigree of Jesus the Messiah!

Why include these four in the list? Because these four reveal the nature of the New Creation, and they reveal the heart of Him who is the new creation. Specifically, the inclusion of the four women in Jesus' pedigree tells us that the New Creation overcomes all the barriers which divide the old creation. In the New Creation, all the walls of the old come down!

The inclusion of the women says that Jesus Christ overcomes the barrier between male and female. It may have been unusual for women to be included in the genealogy of the men of the old order, but it is not unusual for women to be included in the genealogy of The Man of the new order. Right from the beginning of his Gospel, Matthew signals what he makes more explicit as the rest unfolds; namely, that to Jesus Christ, women are not pieces of property, but persons. Jesus Christ, the New Creation, gives women dignity.

The inclusion of these four also says that Jesus Christ overcomes the barrier between Jew and Gentile. There was no greater racial-ethnic barrier. Jewish genealogies were written to prove that one was free of Gentile contamination. Yet there they are! Gentiles in the pedigree of the New Creation. Gentile blood runs in the veins of the Jewish Messiah! Interracial, multi-cultural blood flows in the veins of the Son of David, Son of Abraham.

The inclusion of these four names also announces the coming down of yet another wall, the biggest, tallest, thickest wall of all. Jesus Christ overcomes the barrier between the Holy God and unholy humanity. All four women are unholy sinners, yet here they are in the pedigree of the Holy One, the Sin-less One! The four women are of course not the only sinners in the list – every man in this list is a sinner! Abraham was hardly a saint; the same is true of Isaac and Jacob and Judah. Tamar was able to seduce Judah her father-in-law because he was out looking for a one-night stand. And King David, the "man after God's own heart" was hardly pure. It was he, not Bathsheba, who initiated their affair. Every single person in the gene pool of Jesus is a sinner: Asa, Ahaz, Manasseh – proud, arrogant, greedy, dishonest. Yet there they are in the pedigree of the New Adam.

Right from the start of his Gospel, Matthew signals what he makes explicit as the rest unfolds: the child is born for sinners. He is born for me! He comes through the sinful, to identify with the sinful, to rescue the sinful from their sins. That is why His name is Jesus, Matthew says in the paragraph following the genealogy, "for He will save His people from their sins" (Matthew 1:21).

That is what the genealogy is announcing. The Advent-Christmas season is for sinners! The new creation is for sinners! For me!

Prayer
Barrier-breaking God,
I come to You today aware of how little
I deserve to approach You,
and in awe, I realize that You have
chosen to draw near to me.
I come to You today confessing my sin,
and in amazement, I acknowledge
that Christmas is for me.
I come to You today aware of my need of a Saviour,
and in joy, I affirm that because of this, Jesus was born.
Continue to break down the barriers in
my heart to truly believing this,
and may I answer Your call to break down the barriers
that I put up which separate me from others. Amen.

Thursday

Christmas is all about the Living God. Christmas is all about what God did. In the face of collapsing moral order and intellectual frameworks, in the face of the hunger and thirst in the human soul, God did something. Yes, so did Mary, and so did Joseph, and so did Caesar Augustus, and sadly, so did King Herod. But the main actor in Christmas is God. God acted. Big time!

And what did God do?

God sent a fleet of blimps, with neon lights flashing "turn or burn!" The night sky was filled with them. Through loud speakers, God yelled, "You miserable creeps . . . you better get your act together or I am going to rain fire on you." Right? No, thank God!

God stirred up the citizens of the empire to elect lawmakers who would cause the Roman Senate to pass and enforce laws friendly to the Jewish value system. Right? No.

God inspired a number of creative people to write little booklets with easy self-help techniques – *One Minute Spirituality* and *Ten Ways to a New You*. What Mary held in her arms on Christmas was a copy of *Seven Steps to Free Yourself from Guilt and Shame*. Right? No.

God created a new institution, with a new rule book, to help keep chaos in check. It is because of the new rule book that the shepherds ran to the manger and worshipped. Right? No.

What did God do?

God sent a Person – His Son. And in sending His Son, God sent Himself. That is Christmas! Let this grab your heart and mind as never before: God gives Himself! In the face of the collapsing moral and intellectual order, in the face of a huge vacuum in the soul of humanity, the Holy God gives Himself.

In the fullness of time, God sends Himself. To immoral people, to rebellious people, to lost people, to dying people . . . God gives Himself! Not a spanking. Not a plague. Not a program. Not an institution. Not a new rule book. Himself. That is Christmas!

Not that a blimp blinking "turn or burn" would not help. It just might. We are playing with fire when we dismantle God's moral order. We will get burned if we do not turn around. We are getting burned.

Not that electing legislators who will pass laws in concert with God's law would not help. It will. As will judges who honour the law behind the law. It is just that law never gives life. Law does not have the inherent power to enable people to obey.

Not that books with principles to live by would not help. They might, and they do for awhile. It is just that principles do not set captives free. With the collapse of the moral order we have become prisoners to forces beneath our created dignity. We need more than principles to live by . . . even godly principles to live by.

The collapse of the moral and intellectual order and the hunger and thirst in the soul can never be healed by law, principles, or institutions. The collapse in the moral order and the hole in the soul are the result of a breakdown in relationship – a breakdown in relationship with the Living God. Healing comes through restoration of the relationship, and only persons can heal relationships.

And so, God sent Himself. To sinful people, to empty people, to hurting people, to real people, in real time, God gives us Himself! That is Christmas.

Prayer

All-powerful God,
though we deserved Your anger and judgment,
though we had no right to good
advice or teaching from You,
though in grace You might have
sent us rules and principles,
You gave us so much more at Christmas
... You gave us Yourself.
May I this day accept the relationship you offer me,
and choose to live in light of that amazing gift. Amen.

Week 2

Friday

Christmas is a time of great joy and celebration. But it is also a time of great sadness. For all the tremendous, good achievements of humanity in medicine, technology, and communications, humankind really hasn't changed. It makes one wonder what really happened in Bethlehem so long ago. Maybe . . . maybe the human spirit so longs for something like the Christmas story that we made it up, dreaming up the incredible story of God coming to earth in order to make sense of our apparently senseless world.

Maybe the Christmas dream is over. Maybe we've sung the carols year after year hoping that if we sing them enough, the dream will come true. I wonder if the shepherds who came to the stable that night felt that the dream was over when a few months later King Herod ordered the murder of all boys two years old and under.

If what the New Testament says about Christmas is true with its talk of redemption and adoption, if this is what Christmas is supposed to accomplish, why hasn't it had a greater impact? Listen to what the apostle John tells us: "He was in the world, and the world was made through Him, and the world did not know Him. He came to His own, and those who were His own did not receive Him" (John 1:10-11).

John tells us a sad fact: when the Son of God came into our world He was not welcomed as He ought. The fact that Mary and Joseph could find no room in Bethlehem's hotels is a parable of the world's feelings for Jesus Christ: very few people will give Him a room. Very few will even let Him in the door for a brief dialogue. King Herod even tried to kill Him.

But John does not end with the sad fact, for he goes on to say: "But as many as received Him, to them He gave the right to become children of God, even to those who believe in His name" (John 1:12).

Christmas becomes a reality in our life when, but only when, we receive the Son of God. The reason Christmas has not yet fulfilled all it was supposed to – all the glory we sing about in the carols – is because so few people have received the Son, even so few who sit in church week after week. That sounds simplistic, I know, but it is the way it is. We are still slaves to our fallen nature until the Son sets us free and makes us children of God.

So what can we do about all of the brokenness around us? We can bring our hurting world the good news, the Christmas news: "The Son has come. Here is our Redeemer. He can set you and me free – He can. Let's give

Him a chance. He can fill you and me with new life – He can. Let's give Him a chance."

When we receive the Son, something happens: there is a new beginning, a new birth, a new vision, a new power to live. The indwelling life of the Son doesn't make us perfect – but it does change us.

I feel sad at Christmas for lots of reasons. I know many people's hurts, and I have my own. But I mostly feel sad because I realize how few people have received the Christ-child. My heart breaks when I go shopping and hear the carols over the loud speakers and then see hundreds of people who don't believe a word of it.

Though I feel great sorrow during Christmas, I can still rejoice in what Christmas is all about: God so loves this fallen, violent world, that He sends His only Son that whoever will receive Him can be freed and adopted into His family.

Prayer

Everlasting God,
it's Advent once again.
We've eagerly waited for change, but
it appears little has happened.
Expand in me the great hope that one day
I will be raised from this broken earth
– changed in the blink of an eye –
and that everything bent and bruised,
curdled and corrupted,
in me and this world, will be transformed
into lasting goodness, righteousness, and truth.
In Jesus' name, amen.

Saturday

Because the Child is born, darkness does not have the last word. Jesus the light shines in the darkness, and as the apostle John declares, "the darkness has not overcome it" (John 1:5, NIV). A number of years ago, the narrator at our children's High School concert put it powerfully: "Never again will there be total darkness."

> The people who walk in darkness
> Will see a great light;
> Those who live in a dark land,
> The light will shine on them.
>
> Isaiah 9:2

Jesus the light breaks the spell of darkness. He exposes the lies and overcomes the illusions. He shines into the suffocating dark of depression. I know . . . He has done it for me.

Isaiah is not saying that darkness eventually gives way to light. He is not holding before us some automatic, evolutionary urge within the cosmos. Left to itself, darkness gets darker. It is because the Child is born that light shines in the darkness. It is because Jesus is Who He is that the darkness can never extinguish the light.

> You shall multiply the nation,
> You shall increase their gladness.

Isaiah 9:3

Because the Child is born, sorrow does not have the last word. Jesus, the joy of God, lifts the heaviness of disappointment and despair. His Presence pushes away the weight of grey gloom.

I know that for many people, this time of the year is a hard time, filled with sadness. And I understand why – it happens to me, too. Look not at the disappointments, nor at the broken expectations, all the needs, or the losses. Rather, look at – look to – the Child. Look at Jesus. When we see Him, His joy breaks through the gloom!

Again, Isaiah is not saying that sorrow eventually gives way to joy. He is not holding before us some automatic, evolutionary urge within the cosmos. Left to itself, sorrow gets worse. It is because the Child is born that joy breaks into the gloom. It is because Jesus is Who He is that mourning can turn into dancing again.

> You shall break the yoke of their burden
> And the staff on their shoulders

Isaiah 9:4

Because the Child is born, oppression – be it political, economic, emotional, or spiritual – does not have the last word. Jesus, the mighty God, the Divine warrior, shatters the yokes! Oh, how we need to hear this in our time. Is not our time a time of terrible bondage? Is not North America held captive, not to a super-power like Assyria, but to a "super-er-power" named Addiction?

Oh, brothers and sisters! Because the child is born, bondage does not have the last word. Because the Son is given, there is hope for freedom from any form of addiction. Jesus the stronger-than-any-"super-er-power" can break the yoke of alcohol, or cocaine, or pornography, or materialism. Jesus the champion can free us from terrifying memories, crippling guilt, bitterness, self-pity, and poor self-esteem. He comes to set the captives free! Sin and Satan lose their grip when Jesus enters the picture.

Once more, Isaiah is not saying that bondage eventually gives way to freedom. He is not holding before us some automatic, evolutionary urge within the cosmos. Left to itself, addiction finally kills. It is because the Child is born that the yoke of oppression is shattered. It is because Jesus is Who He is that the chains fall off.

Darkness is strong . . . I know. But Jesus the Light is stronger.

Sorrow is strong . . . I know. But Jesus the Joy is stronger.

Bondage is strong . . . I know. But Jesus our Freedom is stronger.

Prayer
O God,
we live as if the light had never defeated
the darkness in the world or in us.
We confess that we ignore the Christ
You sent to be among us, to be in us.
We've kept the birth of Your Son
confined to the Christmas season
and do not yearn for His birth each
moment in our waiting hearts.
Lord, You came to us in the fullness of time.
Forgive us for not opening our eyes to Your coming.
It's time that we prepare for Your coming.
Let the earth ring with song. Let the light break forth.
Let us all rejoice in the miracle of love.
Let Christ come into the fullness of our time. Amen.[*]

[*] Adapted from *The Worship Sourcebook* (Grand Rapids: Faith Alive, 2004), 442.

Week 3

Readings

Now the birth of Jesus Christ was as follows: when His mother Mary had been betrothed to Joseph, before they came together she was found to be with child by the Holy Spirit. And Joseph her husband, being a righteous man and not wanting to disgrace her, planned to send her away secretly. But when he had considered this, behold, an angel of the Lord appeared to him in a dream, saying, "Joseph, son of David, do not be afraid to take Mary as your wife; for the Child who has been conceived in her is of the Holy Spirit. She will bear a Son; and you shall call His name Jesus, for He will save His people from their sins." Now all this took place to fulfill what was spoken by the Lord through the prophet: "BEHOLD, THE VIRGIN SHALL BE WITH CHILD AND SHALL BEAR A SON, AND THEY SHALL CALL HIS NAME IMMANUEL," which translated means, "GOD WITH US." And Joseph awoke from his sleep and did as the angel of the Lord commanded him, and took Mary as his wife, but kept her a virgin until she gave birth to a Son; and he called His name Jesus.

Matthew 1:18-25

Now in those days a decree went out from Caesar Augustus, that a census be taken of all the inhabited earth. This was the first census taken while Quirinius was governor of Syria. And everyone was on his way to register for the census, each to his own city. Joseph also went up from Galilee, from the city of Nazareth, to Judea, to the city of David which is called Bethlehem, because he was of the house and family of David, in order to register along with Mary, who was engaged to him, and was with child. While they were there, the days were completed for her to give birth. And she gave birth to her firstborn son; and she wrapped Him in cloths, and laid Him in a manger, because there was no room for them in the inn.

In the same region there were some shepherds staying out in the fields and keeping watch over their flock by night. And an angel of the Lord suddenly stood before them, and the glory of the Lord shone around them; and they were terribly frightened. But the angel said to them, "Do not be afraid; for behold, I bring you good news of great joy which will be for all the people; for today in the city of David there has been born for you a Savior, who is Christ the Lord. This will be a sign for you: you will find a baby wrapped in cloths and lying in a manger." And suddenly there appeared with the angel a multitude of the heavenly host praising God and saying,

"Glory to God in the highest,

And on earth peace among men with whom He is pleased."

When the angels had gone away from them into heaven, the shepherds began saying to one another, "Let us go straight to Bethlehem then, and see this thing that has happened which the Lord has made known to us." So they came in a hurry and found their way to Mary and Joseph, and the baby as He lay in the manger. When they had seen this, they made known the statement which had been told them about this Child. And all who heard it wondered at the things which were told them by the shepherds. But Mary treasured all these things, pondering them in her heart. The shepherds went back, glorifying and praising God for all that they had heard and seen, just as had been told them.

And when eight days had passed, before His circumcision, His name was then called Jesus, the name given by the angel before He was conceived in the womb.

Luke 2:1-21

Week 3

Sunday

Spending time with Joseph is a bit more difficult than spending time with Mary, because Joseph does not say much in the drama. In fact, Joseph does not say anything at all in the Christmas story! Yet, like many gentle, quiet types, his actions speak volumes.

We first meet Joseph when he is betrothed to a lovely, young lady. In the first century, getting married involved three steps. The first was engagement, a formal ceremony in which you promise yourself to one another. The second step was betrothal, a legally binding step. After declaring your intentions, you live apart for about a year. You are legally husband and wife, but not yet sharing the same house and bed. The third stage is the wedding service, when the whole village gathers to celebrate and bless the couple.

During the betrothal stage, Joseph would have been caught up in all the physical and emotional energy of preparing a new home for his bride-to-be. He would have been alive with expectations and longings, fantasizing of love and happiness, and counting the days until he could bring Mary home. And then came the shocking news: Mary was pregnant. Joseph would be stunned . . . and deeply hurt.

The only explanation was that Mary had not been faithful to her vow – she had cheated on Joseph. Those who have been deserted or betrayed by someone they trusted know a little of what Joseph was feeling: raw, unalloyed pain.

Matthew tells us that Joseph was "a righteous man" (Matthew 1:19). This is a technical term in the first century, meaning that he was a man who was faithful to all his relationships, especially to his relationship with the living God and God's will as it is expressed in God's law. Joseph was a "right-relationship" man.

Now, according to the law, when a woman is unfaithful she is to be taken to the court and openly exposed for breaking the legal bond. As Joseph, the "righteous man" struggles with his pain, he chooses not to exercise this legal right. Although he seeks a right relationship with the law, he also seeks a right relationship with Mary. He does not want to shame her. What good would that do?

While wrestling with what to do next, an angel of the Lord appears to Joseph in a dream. And this is one of the things that Joseph can remind us: the Living God communicates with His people. If we seek to do the righteous thing, if we earnestly seek to be right with God and with others, God will come to us in our wrestling and guide us into "paths of righteousness" (Psalm 23:3).

God does this most clearly through the study of Scripture. God also does this through the wise counsel of Godly elders. God does it through the words of trusted friends. And, God does it through dreams.

God did this for Joseph four times in the Christmas Story. First, to explain Mary's pregnancy (Matthew 1:20-21); second, to tell him to flee to Egypt from Herod's mass extermination program (Matthew 2:13); third, to let him know it was safe to return to Palestine (Matthew 2:19-20); and fourth, to warn him to stay away from Judea, and return to Galilee (Matthew 2:22-23). The point is that the Living God will meet us in our seeking after righteousness . . . even in our dreams!

We need to listen to our dreams, especially those that involve discipleship issues. Yes, most dreams emerge from our deep longings or fears, or are the replay of the TV program we watched before going to sleep. But once in a while, they just may be God graciously communicating with us.

Whatever you make of it all, hang on to this: Joseph's experience tells us that our God does not want us to linger in confusion. The Living God communicates and guides. "I am the Light of the world," says Jesus; the one "who follows Me will not walk in the darkness, but will have the Light of life" (John 8:12).

Prayer

Lord, we thank You that You are the God who speaks.
In the beginning, in the midst of formless emptiness,
You spoke into the darkness and
created a world of wonders.
In the fullness of time, in the midst
of our sin and brokenness,
You spoke into the darkness and Jesus
was born into our world.
And in the present, in the midst of
our muddled confusion,
You speak into our lives, and lead us in right paths.
May my ears be attentive to Your voice today,
and may I recognize and obey the
guidance You provide. Amen.

Week 3

Monday

Names in the first century meant so much more than they do in our time. A person's name was carefully chosen, for the name was intended to make a statement, a statement about the person's essential self. A name was a sort of mini personality profile, a kind of character reference. "Joseph . . . you shall give the Spirit-begotten child the name Jesus . . . His name shall be called Immanuel."

"Jesus," an ordinary human name. Many mothers in the first century gave their sons that name; many mothers still do. "Jesus" is the English for the Greek *Iesuos*. *Iesous* is the Greek for the Hebrew *Yeshua*, often translated as Joshua. And here is the fact we need to know to appreciate what is going on in the naming of Mary's son: *Yeshua* is a short form of *Ye-ho-shuah*, which means "Yahweh is the One who saves." More dynamically, "Yahweh-to-the-rescue!" You shall give Him the name "Yahweh-to-the-rescue."

Now, other children bearing this name were signs, or statements of faith, that God saves. What Matthew is wanting us to know about this Yeshua, this boy, is that He is not just a sign; He is the thing signified. This Yeshua, literally, "out of the Spirit of Yahweh," is somehow Yahweh in person; He is literally Yahweh-to-the-rescue!

That Matthew intends for us to think in this way is made clear by the explanation for giving Jesus this name. Matthew reports the angel saying, and here I will translate literally, "You are to give Him the name Jesus, because He Himself will save His people from their sins" (Matthew 1:21). "He Himself, He Himself will save . . . ." Who is this "Himself"? Who is this person who is Himself the Saviour of His people?

Over and over again, God says through the Jewish prophets, "I, even I, am Yahweh; and there is no savior besides me" (e.g., Isaiah 43:11). Only God can save, only the Creator can redeem. "You are to give Mary's baby the name Jesus, because He Himself will save . . . ." The angel can make such a startling statement because this Jesus, this Yeshua, is the one Jesus who is in fact what His name means. This Jesus is in the most literal sense of the word "Yahweh Himself to the rescue."

And He is to be named "Immanuel." Other mothers called their children by this name too, and still do. Matthew quotes Isaiah, who spoke of some child in Isaiah's time who was given this name. But again, that child was only a sign, a statement of faith, that somehow God-is-with-us. But *this* child, Mary's boy-child, is not just a sign, He is the thing signified. Because He is "of the Spirit of

God," "out of the Spirit of God," He is God-in-Person, God-with-us. Or as both the Hebrew and Greek should be rendered, he is the with-us-God. *Immanu* means "with-us." *El* means God! His name is not El-Immanu, but Immanu-El. He is the with-us-God.

I will never tire of proclaiming the wonder and mystery of the names. "Give Him the name Jesus, Immanuel. Give Him the name Yahweh-to-the-rescue, the with-us God." The names declare the incredibly good news that the Living God has come to us in person!!!

I like how the Nicene Creed expresses it: "I believe in one Lord Jesus Christ . . . God of God, Light of light, very God of very God . . . Who for us and our salvation came down . . . and was incarnate by the Holy Spirit of the Virgin Mary." The good news is not simply that the Invisible One has come to us in Jesus of Nazareth. The good news is that the Invisible One has come to us as Jesus of Nazareth. As Jesus! Martin Luther could therefore say: "I know of no God but this one in the manger.'" "Name Him Jesus, Immanuel; Yahweh-Himself-to-the-rescue, the with-us-God."

* As given in Norman E. Nagel, "Martinus: 'Heresy, Doctor Luther, Heresy!' The Person and Work of Christ," in *Seven-Headed Luther: Essays in Commemoration of a Quincentenary 1483-1983*, ed. Peter Newman Brooks (Oxford: Clarendon Press, 1983), 48.

Prayer

Eternal Father,
we give thanks for Your incarnate Son,
whose name is our salvation.
Plant in every heart, we pray,
the love of Him who is the Saviour of the world,
our Lord Jesus Christ;
who lives and reigns with You and the Holy Spirit,
one God, in glory everlasting. Amen.[*]

* *The Book of Alternative Services of the Anglican Church of Canada*
(Toronto: Anglican Book Centre, 1985), 277.

WEEK 3

Tuesday

Matthew puts the story of the namings at the beginning of the Gospel to make sure we read the rest of his Gospel correctly. That is, Matthew intends for us to read the rest of what he writes through the lens of the names. As we turn the pages of his book and watch Mary's Son relate to real people in real life situations, we are to say to ourselves, "This is Yahweh-Himself-to-the-rescue doing this," "this is the with-us-God doing that."

When we read the Gospels through the lens of the names, we discover that God embraces and identifies with the pains, struggles and hurts of our world. But He does more than this: God feels the realities of life on this planet. The Living God feels. The Invisible One feels. This is truly astounding!

Most religions affirm four major attributes of God: that God is infinite, incomprehensible, invisible, and impassible, non-feeling. As the Greeks put it, God is a-pathetic, non-passionate. In the Greek philosophical tradition, which has influenced much of Western Christianity, God cannot feel because it would mean that God can be affected by something outside God's Self. In the Greek philosophical tradition, God must not be moved by anything else, for that would, in the Greek mind, imply that God is somehow subject to reality outside God's Self.

Therefore, God, to be God, cannot experience emotions whether pleasant or painful. To feel would mean being less that the Absolute. The Buddhist tradition never attributes "feeling" to the Divine. To feel is to still be caught up in the "veil of illusions." The Islamic tradition holds the view of a non-feeling God. When a Muslim suffers, he or she suffers for Allah, but never with Allah.

When the living God enters the world through the virgin's womb, God breaks open all the philosophical and religious boxes and feels. God voluntarily embraces, voluntarily identifies with, and voluntarily feels the realities of our lives.* The God of Advent-Christmas feels for and feels with.

Matthew uses a strong word to convey the level at which God-with-us feels. It is the word *splangkna,* a visceral word too weakly translated as "compassion." It is the word translated in other Biblical texts as "bowels" or "guts." It refers to the inner parts of our bodies where we feel our deepest and most intense emotions. The *splangkna*

* I owe the "voluntarily" to Jurgen Moltmann.

are the places where we experience those emotions that clutch at us, that wrench and rip.

Read the Gospels through the lens of the names! There He is, Yahweh-to-the- rescue, wrenched by the masses of people aimlessly wandering like sheep without a shepherd (Matthew 9:36). There He is, the-with-us-God, torn up by the grief of a widow on her way to bury her dead son (Luke 7:13). Jesus responds the way He does, not to prove He is Immanuel, but because *as* Immanuel, He feels the pain.

There He is, God-with-us at the grave of His good friend Lazarus. Immanuel stands at the grave. So deeply moved, as John tells it, that He weeps uncontrollably (John 11:33-35). The verb "deeply moved" is another vivid, visceral word. It docs not simply mean to feel sorry. Literally it means, "to snort in spirit." In classical Greek, it was used to describe a horse preparing to enter into battle, rearing up on its front legs, pawing in the air, snorting. At the grave of Lazarus, Yahweh-to-the-rescue snorts in spirit.

Os Guinness captures it best:

> He [Jesus] was moved deeply in the sense of a furious inner anger. Entering his Father's world as the Son of God, he found not order, beauty, harmony and fulfillment, but fractured disorder, raw ugliness, complete disarray – everywhere the abortion of God's original plan. Standing at the graveside, he came face to face

93

with a death that symbolized and summarized the accumulation of evil, pain, sorrow, suffering, injustice, cruelty and despair. Thus while he was moved to tears for his friends in sorrow, he was also deeply moved by the outrageous abnormality of death.[*]

Immanuel's heart breaks with what breaks ours.

Prayer

O Jesus, who wept over the death of
Lazarus, be with all who grieve.
O Jesus, who wept over the state of Jerusalem,
be with our cities, our villages, and our centers of worship.
O Jesus, who wept alone in Gethsemane,
be with all who feel alone, all who face difficult decisions.
O Jesus, who cried "My God, my God,
why have you forsaken me?"
be with all who are tortured, all who are victims.
O Jesus, who offered up prayers with loud cries and tears,
hear our prayers....
O Jesus, who wept in sympathy and frustration,
O living God, who knows all our pain and joy,
be with us in our lives. Amen.

---

[*] Os Guinness, *The Dust of Death: A Critique of the Establishment and the Counter Culture – and a Proposal for a Third Way* (Downers Grove: InterVarsity, 1973), 385.

Wednesday

At every major turning point in the Christmas story, an angel shows up. Four times an angel suddenly appears . . . and speaks. To Zacharias, to Mary, to Joseph (repeatedly!), and to the shepherds.

Four times an angel steps forward and speaks. And each time, the angel begins, "Do not be afraid!" Why? Partly because an encounter with a heavenly messenger should trigger a certain level of fright! But mostly because "do not be afraid" is the major exhortation of the Christmas story. God is doing something in the birth of Jesus that addresses our fears.

To Zacharias, the temple priest: "Do not be afraid . . . your petition has been heard" (Luke 1:13). For years he and his wife Elizabeth prayed for the ability to conceive, and with each passing year the possibility of conception became less and less likely. Then, out of the blue, an angel finds Zacharias going about his sacred duties and tells him that all along his and Elizabeth's prayers were not simply bouncing off the ceiling . . . their prayers have been heard. And so have yours, and so have mine.

To Mary, the virgin: "Do not be afraid . . . nothing will be impossible with God" (Luke 1:30, 37). She too had been minding her business, going about her normal routines, when, out of the blue, an angel finds her and tells her she will conceive and bear a son. "How can this be, since I am a virgin?" "Nothing is impossible with God" – not even this. And not even what you are facing, or what I am facing.

To the shepherds: "Do not be afraid . . . there has been born for you a Savior" (Luke 2:10-11). A Saviour: someone who can recue you from the power and devastation of sin. Sin will no longer have the last word! Oppression and injustice will no longer have the last word – for the shepherds, for the magi, for the first disciples, for you, and for me.

And to Joseph: "Do not be afraid to take Mary as your wife; for the Child who has been conceived in her is of the Holy Spirit" (Matthew 1:20). Joseph had, like many of us, written the script for his future: Finish the apartment in his father's house, pay off the wedding bills, learn to be a faithful husband, increase productivity at the shop, obtain better quality lumber from Lebanon, save for the children's education, accept the invitation to be an elder in the synagogue . . . . The future was straightforward, predictable, and manageable. And then the news . . . one word . . . "pregnant." Not just unsettling – devastating.

Then the angel appears in a dream – as happened to the other Joseph in Scripture, Joseph, son of Jacob. "Do not be afraid to take Mary as your wife; for the Child who has been conceived in her is of the Holy Spirit." Mary has not been unfaithful. The strange, unsettling thing happening to Joseph's future is of the Holy Spirit.

Reference to the Holy Spirit would bring Joseph's mind back to creation, when in the beginning, the Holy Spirit hovered over the formless, empty void, and out of that void brought forth the world. Joseph is being told that something like what happened at the beginning is happening again. The same creative Spirit has hovered over the void of Mary's womb, and out of that void is bringing forth a new creation!

Do not be afraid . . . your prayers have been heard.

Do not be afraid . . . nothing is impossible with God.

Do not be afraid . . . there is a Saviour for you.

Do not be afraid . . . the strange, unsettling thing happening in your life just might be due to Christ's being formed in you and those around you.

Prayer

All glory to You, great God,
for the gift of Your Son,
light in darkness and hope of the world,
whom You sent to save us.
With singing angels
let us praise Your name
and tell the earth His story
that all may believe, rejoice, and bow down,
acknowledging Your love
through Jesus Christ, our Lord. Amen.*

* *The Worship Sourcebook* (Grand Rapids: Faith Alive, 2004), 468-69.

Thursday

The Christmas story does not begin "once upon a time." Fairy tales and myths can begin "once upon a time," but not Christmas. It begins, "In the days of Herod, king of Judea" (Luke 1:5). "Now in those [dateable] days a decree went out from Caesar Augustus, that a census be taken of all the inhabited earth. This was the first census taken while Quirinius was governor of Syria" (Luke 2:1-2).

The Christmas story is told in reference to concrete dates, places, and people, because the great wonder of Christmas takes place in real time and real space. What God did at Christmas, God did in real time. Other stories can disconnect their message from concrete history, but not Christmas.

Christmas is not just the grandest of all fairy tales. I know there are times when it feels like a fairy tale, when the story gets sentimentalized right out of objective history, and therefore seems to have no real relevance. But Christmas takes place in real time, thank God!

I remember a disturbing conversation I had with a professor of religion while we were living in Sacramento, California. He had been attending the church I was serving, a church virtually across the street from the University, but he had become more and more uncomfortable with my constant focus on Jesus of Nazareth. He could handle me speaking about "the Living Christ" or "the Holy One," but he bristled when I spoke of knowing and loving Jesus of Nazareth. He and his wife left the church towards the end of my preaching on Jesus' Sermon on the Mount.

On one Saturday morning we ran into each other in a hardware store, and he said to me, "Darrell, the reason we changed churches is that you tie the truths of the Sermon on the Mount too tightly to Jesus of Nazareth." "What's wrong with that?" I asked. "What you need to realize," he answered, "is that even if there were no Jesus of Nazareth, the teachings of the Sermon on the Mount would still be valid for Christian ethics." To which I responded, "We would not even begin to understand the Sermon on the Mount unless we could see it enfleshed in the Preacher on the Mount. There would be no Christian ethics unless it had first been embodied in the historical Jesus. If there were no Jesus of Nazareth, there is no Living Christ . . . there is no Christianity."

In the days of Herod, King of Judea, Augustus, Emperor of Rome, and Quirinius, Governor of Syria . . . . In those days . . . objective dates, objective places, objective people. No Herod, no Augustus, no Quirinius, no Mary, no Joseph, no angels, no shepherds, no Bethlehem, no Nazareth . . . no gospel, no good news. Oh, there still might be good advice, but no good news. Christmas is not a bunch of good advice, but good news – because something happened in real time.

Caesar Augustus really lived, and really ruled over a real empire. According to one biblical scholar, when Augustus became concerned about a decline in the birthrate, he employed both the stick (a crack-down on abortion) and a carrot (tax incentives for big families). "To see if his policies were effective, he took a census of his empire now and then."* And it was during one such real census that Mary and Joseph were forced to travel from Nazareth in Galilee to Bethlehem in Judea. Real people. Real cities. Real time.

Now, it turns out that, unknown to Caesar Augustus and Herod and Quirinius, something more, something bigger, was happening. Someone else was at work, using the census for His greater purposes. But God was at work in real time, in real places, with real people – just as He is today, where you are, and with you and the people around you.

* T. R. Reid and James L. Stanfield, "The Power and Glory of the Roman Empire," *National Geographic* (July 1997).

Prayer

You are the God who works
in real time, in real places, with real people.
I confess that often I don't expect You to work
in my real time,
in my real place,
and with the real people around me
– or the real person that is me!
Open my eyes to what You are doing in my life today,
expand my faith in Your sovereignty,
and may I look for ways to cooperate with You
in what You are doing,
for the sake of Your glory. Amen.

•

WEEK 3

Friday

Although they have been highly romanticized in Christian tradition, in the first century shepherds were the most despised people in society. Although at one time their calling held an honorable place within the life of the covenant people of God (after all, the greatest of the Kings, King David, was a shepherd whose most famous Psalm celebrates God as Shepherd), they were considered to be the lowest of the low. Nothing paid less than shepherding. Good people did not want to be seen with them; it was considered unsafe to be around them.

Luke's telling of the Christmas events is therefore quite shocking to first-century readers. Shepherds, the despised, the ostracized, the "unclean," were the first to hear the good news of Christmas? Of all the people in Palestine, only they get to hear the song of the angels? What a privilege! Let's take a closer look at the shepherds and see what they can teach us about being disciples of Jesus Christ.

First and foremost, they remind us that discipleship is grounded in grace. The shepherds, who could never have measured up to all the rabbinic standards of holiness, discover that they are brought into "the new thing God is doing" simply by grace. Nothing more, nothing less. They whom the religious society has ostracized have found favour with God simply by grace.

I am sure you have felt what I often feel, that my careless comments or thoughtless actions have disqualified me from the Kingdom. It is then that the shepherds in the field preach to me: "For you. I bring *you* good news that shall be for all the people. There has been born *for you* a Saviour." For me?

Second, the shepherds' experience illustrates the great reversal of grace. Jesus would later say, "Many who are first will be last; and the last first" (Matthew 19:30; Mark 10:31). The shepherds near Bethlehem are exhibit A. The bottom of the ladder receives the gospel first.

We here discover that the Living God has a special burden for the marginalized. Not that God does not care for the rich or powerful; that God goes out of the way to reach the wise men clearly suggests the opposite. It's just that God has a unique concern for those on the bottom of any social ladder. (Remember Mary's song in Luke 1:46-53!)

Third, the shepherds teach us that the bottom of the ladder is the place where we meet the Living God. Christmas says we need not climb the ladder to get to God. Christmas says God comes down the ladder to get to us.

And He stays there. God stays down where we are. Climb the ladder if you want ... climb as high as you want, you will not find the Holy One there. The Living God has come down, down where we can meet Him (Philippians 2:5-11). The Living God keeps coming down, and keeps giving Himself away in servant love, and so must we. If we are to know the true God, the God and Father of our Lord Jesus Christ, we must meet Him where He chooses to live, on the bottom rung of the ladder.

Fourth, the shepherds got in on Christmas because they knew they needed something like Christmas, they knew they needed help. They didn't play the religious games that the respectable folks played. The shepherds could see all the wreckage around them and in them, and they knew they needed help from outside themselves.

"Do not be afraid . . . for today in the city of David there has been born for you a Savior" (Luke 2:10-11). The shepherds knew they needed a Saviour ... and they found Him! They found the Great Shepherd, who for them became the Lamb of God who takes away the sin of the world.

Fifth, the shepherds teach us that when we find the Saviour, our lives are marked by joy and gratitude (Luke 2:20). That is not to say there is no more pain, sorrow, or frustration. After all, the shepherds go back to shepherding, and therefore to being ostracized by society. But mixed into it all, moving through it all, is the bass note of joy and gratitude, because grace always engenders joy and gratitude.

When joy is absent, and when gratitude is gone, it's time to get back to Bethlehem, to the manger, to where we find grace again. "For you ... a Saviour ... Christ, the Lord."

Prayer

Jesus is the Word made flesh in our midst.
May His incarnation fill our hearts with joy and peace.
O Lord, give us peace.
Jesus is the promised Savior, born of Mary.
May His birth among us renew our hope.
O Lord, give us hope.
Jesus is the King of kings and the Lord of lords.
May the gift of His presence bring forth rejoicing.
O Lord, give us joy.
Almighty God, Father, Son, and Holy Spirit,
bless us now and forever. Amen.

Week 3

Saturday

For nine months, Mary carried Jesus in her womb. For years afterwards, she would carry Him in her arms and in her heart. It is she who nurses Jesus in infancy. It is Mary who will get up at night to care for Him when He cries. It is she who will change His diapers and wash His clothes. It is she who will be there when Jesus takes His first steps, and will put bandages on His first cuts. It is she who will teach Him how to speak, and how to pray. It is Mary who gives Him His facial features. People will look at Jesus and say to Mary, "My, how He looks like you!"

Luke says of Jesus' mother: "But Mary treasured all these things, pondering them in her heart" (Luke 2:19). The word Dr. Luke uses means "to confer with," or more literally, "to put together." Mary is taking in all that had been said about her Baby, "conferring" within herself, and trying to put it all together.

She is just a teenager, over a hundred kilometers from home in a strange town. She is resting on a bed of straw in a stable, a shelter built to house farm animals, and she has just given birth – without the help of a doctor, without the assistance of a mid-wife, and without the comforting presence of her mother. She is exhausted. Yet, like most new mothers, she is thrilled! She is fully sore, yet, along with Joseph, caught up in the sense of wonder filling the whole stable. What is she thinking that night? What is she feeling that evening? What did Mary know on that first Christmas?

Maybe she was trying to put together the words she heard nine months earlier, processing all that the angel had said that day in Nazareth, when she was told she will become pregnant: "You will conceive in your womb and bear a son, . . . He will be great and will be called the Son of the Most High; and the Lord God will give Him the throne of His father David; and He will reign over the house of Jacob forever, and His kingdom will have no end" (Luke 1:31-33). My baby, Son of the Most High? My child, Ruler on the throne of David? This little boy, King over a kingdom that will never end?

Or, maybe she was trying to put together the words Joseph shared with her. Maybe she was processing all the angel had told him when Joseph learned she was pregnant, when the angel told him not to be afraid, for what was happening in Mary's womb was a new creative work of the Living God.

Maybe Mary was trying to put together the words the shepherds had joyfully announced when they had come to the stable. Perfect strangers (and smelly strangers at that!), with the news that a whole host of angels had met them saying, "Today in the city of David there has been born for you a Savior, who is Christ the Lord" (Luke 2:11). Saviour? Messiah? Lord? This little child?

Did Mary know that her little baby was all of this? Did she understand what she was holding as she carried her son? How could she know? She was trying to put it all together, but it took decades for the early church to finally understand who Jesus is and what His birth means for the world. It would take centuries more for the church to articulate the contours of the mystery: the Maker of all things in the arms of a teenage girl! The Creator of everything at the mercy of His creatures? And the question shifts, from "Did Mary know?" to "Do I know?" and "Do you know?"

Do you know that the lips of the Child in the manger once spoke the universe into being? Do you know that the Child in the stable spoke humans into being, and made you? Do you know that it was Mary's Son who has come into your world to rescue you from all that keeps you from being who He designed you to be?

Do you know that the sleeping Baby of Christmas would, as He grew into adulthood, bring heaven down to earth? That He would cause the kingdom of heaven to break into the kingdom of earth? Do you know that Mary's child would one day die on a Roman cross, and that His blood would cover the sin of the world? Do you know that in Mary's Son dying on that cross, death would meet its match, and that because He dies we live?

Do you know that Mary's Son delights in you? That He is for you? That He is with you? That He wants to live in you? Do you know? Do you know that as tenderly as Mary held Jesus that first Christmas, it is nothing compared to how tenderly He holds you? Do you know that once He takes hold of you, He will never let you go?

Do you know?

Prayer
Father God,
out of your glorious riches strengthen me with power
through Your Spirit in my inner being,
so that Christ may dwell in my heart through faith.
And may I, rooted and established in love,
have power, together with all the Lord's holy people,
to grasp how wide and long and high
and deep is the love of Christ,
and to know this love that surpasses knowledge –
that I may be filled to the measure of
all the fullness of God. Amen.

WEEK 4

Readings

And when the days for their purification according to the law of Moses were completed, they brought Him up to Jerusalem to present Him to the Lord (as it is written in the Law of the Lord, "Every firstborn male that opens the womb shall be called holy to the Lord"), and to offer a sacrifice according to what was said in the Law of the Lord, "A pair of turtledoves or two young pigeons."

And there was a man in Jerusalem whose name was Simeon; and this man was righteous and devout, looking for the consolation of Israel; and the Holy Spirit was upon him. And it had been revealed to him by the Holy Spirit that he would not see death before he had seen the Lord's Christ. And he came in the Spirit into the temple; and when the parents brought in the child Jesus, to carry out for Him the custom of the Law, then he took Him into his arms, and blessed God, and said,

"Now Lord, You are releasing Your bond-servant to depart in peace,
According to Your word;

For my eyes have seen Your salvation,
Which You have prepared in the presence of all
peoples,
A Light of revelation to the Gentiles,
And the glory of Your people Israel."

And His father and mother were amazed at the things which were being said about Him. And Simeon blessed them and said to Mary His mother, "Behold, this Child is appointed for the fall and rise of many in Israel, and for a sign to be opposed – and a sword will pierce even your own soul – to the end that thoughts from many hearts may be revealed."

And there was a prophetess, Anna the daughter of Phanuel, of the tribe of Asher. She was advanced in years and had lived with her husband seven years after her marriage, and then as a widow to the age of eighty-four. She never left the temple, serving night and day with fastings and prayers. At that very moment she came up and began giving thanks to God, and continued to speak of Him to all those who were looking for the redemption of Jerusalem.

When they had performed everything according to the Law of the Lord, they returned to Galilee, to their own city of Nazareth. The Child continued to grow and become strong, increasing in wisdom; and the grace of God was upon Him.

Luke 2:22-40

Now after Jesus was born in Bethlehem of Judea in the days of Herod the king, magi from the east arrived in Jerusalem, saying, "Where is He who has been born King of the Jews? For we saw His star in the east and have come to worship Him." When Herod the king heard this, he was troubled, and all Jerusalem with him. Gathering together all the chief priests and scribes of the people, he inquired of them where the Messiah was to be born. They said to him, "In Bethlehem of Judea; for this is what has been written by the prophet:

'AND YOU, BETHLEHEM, LAND OF JUDAH,
ARE BY NO MEANS LEAST AMONG THE LEADERS OF
JUDAH;
FOR OUT OF YOU SHALL COME FORTH A RULER
WHO WILL SHEPHERD MY PEOPLE ISRAEL.'"

Then Herod secretly called the magi and determined from them the exact time the star appeared. And he sent them to Bethlehem and said, "Go and search carefully for the Child; and when you have found Him, report to me, so that I too may come and worship Him." After hearing the king, they went their way; and the star, which they had seen in the east, went on before them until it came and stood over the place where the Child was. When they saw the star, they rejoiced exceedingly with great joy. After coming into the house they saw the Child with Mary His mother; and they fell to the ground and worshiped Him. Then, opening their treasures, they presented to Him gifts of gold, frankincense, and myrrh. And having been warned by God in a dream not to return to Herod, the magi left for their own country by another way.

Now when they had gone, behold, an angel of the Lord appeared to Joseph in a dream and said, "Get up! Take the Child and His mother and flee to Egypt, and remain there until I tell you; for Herod is going to search for the Child to destroy Him."

So Joseph got up and took the Child and His mother while it was still night, and left for Egypt. He remained there until the death of Herod. This was to fulfill what had been spoken by the Lord through the prophet: "Out of Egypt I called My Son."

Then when Herod saw that he had been tricked by the magi, he became very enraged, and sent and slew all the male children who were in Bethlehem and all its vicinity, from two years old and under, according to the time which he had determined from the magi. Then what had been spoken through Jeremiah the prophet was fulfilled:

"A voice was heard in Ramah,
Weeping and great mourning,
Rachel weeping for her children;
And she refused to be comforted,
Because they were no more."

But when Herod died, behold, an angel of the Lord appeared in a dream to Joseph in Egypt, and said, "Get up, take the Child and His mother, and go into the land of Israel; for those who sought the Child's life are dead." So Joseph got up, took the Child and His mother, and came into the land of Israel. But when he heard that Archelaus was reigning over Judea in place of his father Herod, he was afraid to go there. Then after being warned by God in a dream, he left for the regions of Galilee, and came and lived in a city called Nazareth. This was to fulfill what was spoken through the prophets: "He shall be called a Nazarene."

Matthew 2:1-23

Now His parents went to Jerusalem every year at the Feast of the Passover. And when He became twelve, they went up there according to the custom of the Feast; and as they were returning, after spending the full number of days, the boy Jesus stayed behind in Jerusalem. But His parents were unaware of it, but supposed Him to be in the caravan, and went a day's journey; and they began looking for Him among their relatives and acquaintances. When they did not find Him, they returned to Jerusalem looking for Him. Then, after three days they found Him in the temple, sitting in the midst of the teachers, both listening to them and asking them questions. And all who heard Him were amazed at His understanding and His answers. When they saw Him, they were astonished; and His mother said to Him, "Son, why have You treated us this way? Behold, Your father and I have been anxiously looking for You." And He said to them, "Why is it that you were looking for Me? Did you not know that I had to be in My Father's house?" But they did not understand the statement which He had made to them. And He went down with them and came to Nazareth, and He continued in subjection to them; and His mother treasured all these things in her heart.

And Jesus kept increasing in wisdom and stature, and in favor with God and men.

Luke 2:41-52

Sunday

It is so easy to go through the Christmas season and miss the point of it. One person who got it was a man named Simeon. Simeon had eyes to see the point of Christmas.

Simeon sang what he saw in the temple that day: "Now, Lord, You are releasing Your bond-servant to depart in peace, according to Your word; for my eyes have seen Your salvation" (Luke 2:29-30). Simeon had been watching for the rising of what the prophet Malachi called "the sun of righteousness" (Malachi 4:2), for the rising of the Star from the house of Jacob. At last, the wait was over! Simeon sees in the Christmas Child the Bright Morning Star (Revelation 22:16), the star that appears when the night has reached its darkest darkness. Simeon sees in the child all that the child's name implies. Jesus, in Hebrew, Yeshua (Joshua), means "God is salvation," "Yahweh saves," or better yet, "Yahweh to the rescue!"

So Simeon sings his heart out! "My eyes have seen Your salvation, which you have prepared in the presence of all peoples, a light of revelation to the Gentiles, and the glory of Your people Israel" (Luke 2:30-32). Quite a song for a Jewish man to sing! The Child is salvation not only for Israel, but also for Syria and Jordan and Lebanon – for all nations, races, and people groups.

Simeon sees what others in the temple that day missed. He sees that salvation is not a technique or principles to live by. Simeon sees that salvation is a Person. He is looking at a Person when he sings of "God's salvation." Simeon sees that salvation is a particular Person – the One who laid in a manger, hung on a cross, and stood outside an empty tomb.

Simeon sings about a Person. It is in a Person that the world finds peace. It is in a Person that we discover joy. It is in a Person that we experience freedom from addictions. It is in a Person that evil meets its match. It is in a Person that death is overcome. God's salvation of the world is a Person.

And Simeon realizes that God's salvation would precipitate a crisis. How could it be otherwise? Light has come! Some would welcome it, and others would not, for the light uncovers and exposes. "Behold this Child is appointed for the fall and rise of many in Israel, and for a sign to be opposed – and a sword will pierce even your own soul – to the end that thoughts from many hearts may be revealed" (Luke 2:34-35).

Simeon realizes that when the little Child grows up to become a man, He would pose a crisis for everyone He encountered. Again and again the issue would be, "What are you going to do with Me?" We are dealing with One who determines our eternal destiny.

When the Christmas Child became an adult, he offended the prejudices of His people. He lived by standards of right and wrong that challenged theirs, and ours. He called into question the values that shaped their lives. His presence compelled them to renounce their love affairs with lesser gods.

The Child comes to our lives, not to walk with us down the paths we have chosen, but to stand in our way, calling us into His path. He is the Rock upon which we build our lives or over which we trip and fall. Jesus Himself would later say, "Do you suppose that I came to grant peace on Earth? I tell you, no, but rather division; for from now on five members in one household will be divided, three against two and two against three" (Luke 12:51-52). He must have said that with great pain and great sorrow, but that is the way it is. His presence precipitates a crisis: "Are you with Me or against Me?"

Prayer

Blessed are You,
O Lord our God,
for You have sent us Your salvation.
Inspire us by Your Holy Spirit
to recognize Him who is the glory of Israel
and the light for all nations,
Your Son, Jesus Christ, our Lord.
Amen.

WEEK 4

Monday

Why does Simeon see when others in the temple that day did not? Luke tells us that "it had been revealed to him by the Holy Spirit that he would not see death before he had seen the Lord's Christ" (Luke 2:26).

Simeon saw because the Spirit of God had opened his eyes. Simeon was no more intelligent, and no more spiritual, than any of the others gathered in the temple. He saw because he was enabled to see, which is the case for anyone who sees! No one sees the truth about Mary's Child, and His manger, cross, and empty tomb, apart from the regenerative illumination of the Holy Spirit (see 1 Corinthians 12:3).

This raises a very difficult question. Does this mean that the Sprit of God goes around illuminating some, and leaving others in the dark? The word translated "revealed" literally means "a divine response." It can be used to refer to providing an answer to someone who is asking for guidance. In the book of Acts, Luke uses the word to describe God's response to Cornelius the Roman officer's seeking (Acts 10:22).

Simeon was looking, asking, longing for God's salvation. That is, he was open and therefore able to receive the Spirit's illumination. He had recognized his need for salvation; he had admitted his need to be redeemed. And he had realized he could not meet the need himself; his need could only be met "from outside" himself.

Most people do not recognize any need for salvation. Improvement? Of course! But salvation, redemption, rescue? "Not me." Many who recognize a need nevertheless think they can meet it themselves: "I'll pull myself up by my own strength"; "I'll kick that habit on my own."

Who were the ones who failed to see God's salvation in the Child? Who missed the first Christmas? Not the poor, not the outcasts, not "the sinners." They knew they needed a doctor, and they were looking. Those who missed the point of Christmas were those who thought they had it all together – or who thought that given the right circumstances they would get it together.

It was people like Caesar Augustus, too busy carrying the world on his shoulders, too busy controlling the world, his and everyone else's. It was people like the Pharisees and Scribes, too busy being religious. For all their prayers and ritual, they did not really think they needed salvation; those who did thought they could achieve it on their own.

You see, God's coming to the world in and as Jesus Christ says, "I needed to come because you need help," and "I needed to come because you cannot help yourself .

. . you need help from outside yourself . . . you need Me." Those who are seeking, longing, "looking for the consolation of Israel," recognize and welcome the coming!

To others, the coming is an offense – a blow to "the-good-that-is-me." And when they look at the manger or cross or empty tomb, they simply do not see. Simeon had dropped the facades. He had faced himself and his great need. He was, therefore, able to receive the witness of the Holy Spirit that Mary's Son is God's salvation.

Later in Luke's Gospel, Jesus speaks a blessing which, had He been able to speak that day, He would have spoken to Simeon:

"Blessed are the eyes which see the things you see; for I say to you that many prophets and kings wished to see the things which you see, and did not see them, and to hear the things which you hear and did not hear them" (Luke 10:23-24).

What do you see?

Prayer

Lord, it is sobering to remember
that when You appeared on earth in the person of Jesus,
most of the world did not recognize Him
and therefore did not worship Him.
Today we ask for faith that will open our eyes
to see Jesus for who He is,
that we might worship Him in truth.
Open our eyes to see Your glory.
Open our ears to hear Your wisdom.
Open our hands to offer You gifts.
Open our mouths to sing Your praise.
Open our hearts to offer You our love. Amen.

Tuesday

It seems to me that most people who read the story of the magi have the following picture in mind: They see magi from the east being led by a star across the Arabian desert to Palestine. The star is in front of them in the west, step-by-step, leading them westwards. After they arrive in Jerusalem, they learn that they need to go south to Bethlehem. They are then led by the star to Bethlehem, where the star further leads them to the specific neighbourhood and to the specific house where the new-born King lives.

Is that the picture Matthew intends to create in our imaginations? Yes, the magi follow the message of the star, but nowhere does Matthew say, "The star led the wise men." Look carefully at the actual words Matthew uses.

The magi say, "We saw His star in the east, and have come to worship Him" (Matthew 2:2). The magi do not say what we tend to make them say, namely, "While in the east, we saw His star in the west, and have followed it to this place." In fact, they "saw His star in the east" – they were looking the other way! They were looking eastward, away from Palestine.

In verse 7, Herod wants to know "the exact time the star appeared." If the star had appeared in the west, that is, over Palestine, Herod would have certainly seen it, and he would not have needed to ask the question.

After the wise men hear Herod and his advisors, Matthew says they went on their way. And then he says, "The star, which they had seen in the east, went on before them until it came and stood over the place where the Child was" (Matthew 2:9). Again, we read into that sentence the word "led," but is that what Matthew intends us to understand?

"When they saw the star, they rejoiced exceedingly with great joy" (Matthew 2:10). It seems that the wise men were surprised to see the star, the implication being that they had not seen it for some time.

The storyline that Matthew intends to create in our imagination is this: While in an Eastern country, the magi see a new star in the east. They make certain deductions from the star that lead them to turn around and travel thousands of miles in the other direction – to Palestine. As they travel, they are not being led by the star. The star is still in the east, behind them, if you will.

When they get to Palestine, they go to the most logical place, to Jerusalem, to the Royal City. Notice that Matthew does not say the star led them to Jerusalem. Their deductions and the trade routes led them to the City of the King. In Jerusalem, they find out from the Scriptures that the King whose coming they deduced from the star is to be born in Bethlehem. So they begin the five-mile journey to the south. Notice that Matthew says they do so in response to the new data gained from Scripture. They were not, at the beginning of the five-mile journey, following the star. Then, something strange occurs while making the trip to Bethlehem. They noticed that the star that they had seen in the east showed up! It "went on before them," says Matthew (verse 9), until it came to where Jesus was, "and stood over" the house.

The star showed up all of a sudden. It too was going to Bethlehem. Not only toward the village, not only toward the neighbourhood, but to the very place where the Child was . . . and stood right over it. What is going on here?

I think that the star was not guiding the wise men. Matthew never uses the word "guide" or "lead"; that idea is brought to the story by the carols and cards. The star was not leading them . . . it was following. More precisely, the star was being pulled, drawn in. It too was traveling to Bethlehem.

The star was not guiding anyone. The star was there because it was being pulled, drawn in by the infant Jesus. Of course! Ought not the presence of the Creator-as-creature have some kind of effect on the cosmos when He enters creation in person? If the Lord of the Universe has appeared on earth, ought not the created order somehow recognize Him and respond?

Matthew is holding before us the magnetic power of Jesus Christ. There He is, just a helpless infant, and already He is drawing grown men and stars to Himself!

Prayer
Star child,
wanted and welcomed by the humble,
hated and hunted by power-seekers;
refuge and refugee, we love You!
Apple of God's eye,
cherished and chosen by Kingdom-travelers,
rejected and ridiculed by the earth-bound;
sacred and scarred, we honour You!
Light of the world,
tended and treasured by the pure in heart,
shadowed and shunned by the deceitful;
peerless and pierced, we exalt You!

Wednesday

Matthew sets the Arab magi in contrast to Herod, on the one hand, and the chief priests and scribes, on the other. According to William Barclay, these different characters epitomize the world's reaction to the birth of the Divine King.[*]

Herod reacted with great fear that led to intense hostility, because he perceived Jesus to be a threat. Jesus comes into the world to bring abundant life, but that abundant life is experienced only where He is allowed to rule. He is Saviour only where He is allowed to be Lord; He is Redeemer where He is allowed to be Master. Herod had two choices: either get in line with the agenda of the new King, or get rid of the new King. And Herod chose the latter. He wanted to remain in charge of his own life, to be his own lord, and to have the last word.

There have been, and are, many people like Herod. Oh, they may not go to the extreme of wanting to kill Jesus,

---

[*] William Barclay, *The Gospel of Matthew Volume 1 (Chapters 1 to 10)* rev. ed. (Philadelphia: Westminster Press, 1975), 30.

but they do, nevertheless, resent and resist His coming, and they do everything they can to keep Him out of their kingdoms. If we are not willing to come down off the throne and let Jesus be King, we will begin to resent Him and may even become hostile toward Him. King Jesus is a threat to any, great or small, who insist on having it their way.

On the other hand, the chief priests and scribes react with amazing indifference. Of all people, they should have reacted with great enthusiasm. After all, they knew the King was coming. Yet, with all their knowledge, they reacted to the news with cool indifference. They didn't even go with the magi out of curiosity!

Again, there have been, and are, many in the priests and scribes camp. Many have heard the good news all their lives and have grown cold. Week after week, year after year, they hear the message but are never moved. They just keep going on their own way, doing their own thing, living as though the King, by Whose Name they call themselves, never came. I can understand hostility . . . but indifference?

Maybe it's because we have sentimentalized Jesus. Maybe it's because He is so often presented as the meek and mild smiling Galilean whose main concern is to make people feel happy. The sentimentalized Jesus has nothing to do with real life, but not so the real Jesus.

The real Jesus, born in Bethlehem, is the Creator of the Universe, come to live our lives. The real Jesus, born in Bethlehem, is the Re-creator of the Universe, come to re-build our lives. The real Jesus claims to be the Light of the World, the Bread of Life, the Living Water, without which we cannot live. The real Jesus laid down His life for the sins of the world, for the very world that did not receive Him when He came. The real Jesus overcame the power of death – the first person over whom death did not have the last word! The real Jesus has inaugurated a kingdom which "shall stretch from the sun's setting to the sun's rising," a Kingdom that is "higher than the heavens, deeper than the grave."* How can anyone remain apathetic about Him?

In complete contrast to Herod and the priests and scribes, the magi react by seeking the King with all their being. They did something about the good news! They immediately headed off to Bethlehem. They went out of their way to find Jesus Christ. These unnamed pagans, if you will, challenge us. They went way out of their way! They had to travel thousands of miles. There's no telling how long it took to make the trip. There's no telling how much money it cost. We have no way of knowing what

---

* Dorothy Sayers, *The Man Born to Be King* (Grand Rapids: William B. Eerdmans, 1943), 35.

other responsibilities and commitments they had to rearrange or cancel in order to seek the Lord of the Universe.

They went out of their way! Are you and I willing to go out of the way to find him? Are you and I willing to change some of our commitments in order to get to know Him better? Or are we going to wait until seeking the King fits into our schedules? Are we going to wait to deepen our relationship with Him until it is more convenient? It's not that He is far away and we have to travel somewhere else. It's just that, according to Dallas Willard, He ordinarily does not compete for our attention.*

Prayer
Merciful God,
always with us, always coming:
We confess that we do not know
how to prepare for Your Advent.
We have forgotten how to hope in miracles;
we have ignored the promise of Your kingdom;
we get distracted by all the busyness of this season.
Forgive us, God.
Grant us the simple wonder of the shepherds,
the intelligent courage of the Magi,
and the patient faith of Mary and Joseph,
that we may journey with them to Bethlehem
and find the good news of a Child born for us. Amen.

* Dallas Willard, *Hearing God: Developing a Conversational Relationship with God* (Downers Grove: Intervarsity Press, 1984), 90.

Thursday

Matthew goes on to tell us what the magi did once they found Jesus, and I think he is telling us that the same will be true of all who go out of their way to seek him.

First, there is joy. The magi were overwhelmed with joy! Actually, Matthew says, "they rejoiced with exceedingly great joy" (Matthew 2:10). Matthew heaps up all kinds of words and phrases to describe their reaction. "Rejoiced" would be sufficient. But no, he says they "rejoiced with joy." More than that – they "rejoiced with great joy!" Still more than that – they "rejoiced with exceedingly great joy!"

Joy is the emotion that says, "I'm home!" "This is it!" "I've found what've I've always been longing for." This says to me that all homesickness is, finally, homesickness for the King; what we are really aching for is Him. When we find Him, each time we find Him, there is joy.

Second, there is worship. "After coming into the house they saw the Child with Mary His mother Mary; and they fell to the ground and worshipped Him" (Matthew 2:11). What a scene! Grown, educated, wealthy men, on their knees before the Child. But of course! What more appropriate response than with the whole self . . . to fall down. They worshipped the Lord-of-the-Universe-Become-a-Child with their bodies as well as with their minds; with their arms and legs, as well as with their hearts and lips. They worshipped.

Do you worship Jesus? That is the million dollar question. Someone has said that the answer to that question reveals whether or not we understand what really happened at Christmas. The wise men were truly wise; they did not understand everything about the Child, but they did know that He is worthy of the worship given only to the Living God.

Third, there is the opening of the treasure box. "Then, opening their treasures, they presented to Him gifts of gold, frankincense, and myrrh" (Matthew 2:11). Of course! How could they not? He is King, the One Who made us and redeems us for Himself. "Here, Jesus . . . here is my treasure box." Does He have yours?

Gold: a most appropriate gift for a King. Frankincense: the incense of worship, a most appropriate gift for One Who is more than human. Myrrh: an embalming spice, a most appropriate gift for One Who comes to suffer with and die for His people, in order to set them free. The wise men did not understand everything about the Child, but what they did know made them want to open up the treasure box.

And so, too, us. If we really believe He is the King of kings, won't we lay our gold at His feet? Won't we surrender our possessions, our bank accounts, our homes and cars and computers to Him, saying, "Here, use these for your Kingdom"? If we really believe He is the Living God wrapped in our flesh, won't we, like the magi, give Him the incense of adoration? Isn't He worthy of our passionate love? And if we really believe that He is the One Who lays down His life for us, won't we give Him our myrrh . . . our burdens, our sorrows, our tears, and our sickness?

Fourth, there is a new lifestyle. "And having been warned by God in a dream not to return to Herod, the magi left for their own country by another way" (Matthew 2:12). I agree with Dale Bruner, who argues that in Matthew's Gospel the word "way" (or "road") is used in an ethical and theological sense.* Jesus the King would later say in His Sermon on the Mount, " . . . the way is broad that leads to destruction and many are on it . . . . The way is narrow that leads to life and few are those who find it" (Matthew 7:13-14).

Matthew is telling us that the authentic encounter with the King brings joy, and it changes us. Given Who He is, the encounter has to change us. We go back "another way" . . . the way of the Kingdom.

---

* F. Dale Bruner, *The Christbook: A Historical/Theological Commentary (Matthew 1–12)* (Waco, TX: Word Books, 1987 edition), 50.

Prayer

God of gold, we seek Your glory:
the richness that transforms our drabness into color
and brightens our dullness with vibrant light,
Your wonder and joy at the heart of all life.
God of incense, we offer You our prayer:
our spoken and unspeakable longings,
our questioning of truth,
our search for Your mystery deep within
God of myrrh, we cry out to You in our suffering:
the pain of all our rejections and bereavements,
our baffled despair at undeserved suffering,
our rage at continuing injustice.
And we embrace You, God-with-us,
in our wealth, in our yearning, in
our anger and loss. Amen.

WEEK 4

Friday

Christmas reminds us that God identifies with the harsh realities of life on this planet. Christmas points us to Immanuel – the with-us-God. Christmas reminds us of the meaning of the name Jesus – Yahweh-to-the-rescue!

In the Christmas story, we see Yahweh-to-the-rescue emerging from the womb, going through the trauma that is birth. There He is, Immanuel, clutched in the arms of Joseph as he and Mary flee the city, escaping the insane decree of Herod that all boys two-years-old and younger be killed. There He is, the virtuous God, a twelve-year-old boy in trouble with His mother because He sought to understand Himself independent of her and Joseph.

There He is, Yahweh-to-the-rescue, alone in the desert for forty days, hungry and thirsty, in a face-to-face encounter with the powers of evil, being tested more fiercely than any of us ever have or will. There He is, Immanuel, walking into leper colonies, touching the limbs and faces of people whom others dare not touch.

There He is, the with-us-God, laughing, singing, and eating with outcasts, befriending prostitutes and dishonest tax-collectors. There He is, the Holy One, being criticized and jeered at by the religious establishment for such reckless love. There He is in the synagogue, being misunderstood by the theological elite, scorned and hated by the very folk who should have welcomed Him. There He is, exhausted and weary after a long day of teaching.

There He is, Yahweh-Himself-come-to-save, in the garden of Gethsemane, wrestling with having to do what He does not want to do, but knowing that He must do it. There He is, alone, deserted by his friends, agonizing long into the night over the cost of obedience in this world. There He is, in the Roman headquarters, the victim of a miscarriage of justice. There He is, hearing the false testimony against Him being accepted by the court. There He is, God, forced to His knees, being spat upon and whipped by soldiers.

There He is, Yahweh-to-the-rescue, at Golgotha, nails being pounded into His hands and feet, flesh ripping as they drop His cross into the holding place. There He is, He who knew no sin, becoming sin and absorbing in Himself all that sin justly deserves. There He is, dying. God dying! There He is, in the stone cold darkness and silence we call death.

Christmas reminds us that the Living God fully identifies with "the real world," which is why we can trust Him when He speaks to us. He not only knows what He is talking about, He knows what it means to live it out in our world. The Living God knows what it means to be human! God feels the realities of life on this planet.

When the living God enters the world through the virgin's womb, God breaks open all the philosophical and religious boxes. God voluntarily embraces, voluntarily identifies with, and voluntarily feels the realities of our lives.

Christmas reminds us that God is in the hole; He is in the absence. Our Maker bears the grief with us. The Maker of all things bears the grief of the whole world.

This Christmas, embrace all that His name implies. Call Him "Jesus," for He is Yahweh the Holy One, come to rescue us from all the consequences of sin. Call Him "Immanuel," for He is the Eternal Creator come to us as one of us, to be for us the with-us-God . . . now and forevermore.

Prayer

Compassionate God, we come to You in our need
confessing to You what we often
dare not admit to ourselves:
It is hard to celebrate life when faced
with the mystery of death.
It is hard to look to the future when surrounded
by the uncertainty of the present;
it is hard to embrace the day when
hope is eclipsed by despair.
Help us this day to know You and
find You in the whole of life:
its beginnings and its endings,
to discover You in our pain as well as our joy,
in our doubts as well as our believing,
to receive this day, and in the days to come,
comfort from Your word and light for our darkness. Amen.

WEEK 4

Saturday

What do you see this Christmas? Karl Barth once said, "Tell me your Christology and I will tell you who you are."[*] Tell me what you see in the Child in Mary's arms and I will tell you who you are!

May I share with you what I see this Christmas? What I see in Mary's son?

I see in Jesus the fulfillment of promise, and therefore, God's "yes" to all other promises.

I see in Jesus the son of Abraham, the One in whom all nations on earth can be blessed.

I see in Jesus the son of David, the One who establishes and reigns over a Kingdom that has no end.

I see in Jesus the Suffering Servant of Isaiah 53, the One who bears the punishment my sins deserved.

I see in Him the Lamb who takes away the sin of the world.

[*] As given in Colin Gunton, *The Barth Lectures*, Ed. P.H. Brazier (New York: T&T Clark, 2007), 10.

I see in Jesus the Divine made human, the Creator become creature.

I see in Jesus' face the face of the invisible God.

I see in Jesus all we were meant to be . . . and what we, by His grace, shall be.

I see in Jesus God reconciling the world to God's self.

I see the King who can put Humpty Dumpty together again, the One who can repair broken lives.

I see the Prince of Peace, the One who can show the world a way around war if the leaders of the world would just give Him a chance.

I see in Jesus the only One who can satisfy my ravenous hunger and thirst for life.

I see in Jesus the One by whom and for whom I was made.

I see in Jesus the One in whom all things hold together.

I see the One who comes to baptize with the Holy Spirit and fire, who delights in drenching us with, and emerging us in, the purifying life of God.

I see in Jesus the One who breaks the terror of the night, who robs death of its finality.

I see in Jesus the God who paradoxically breaks the stronghold of evil through the weakness and foolishness of the cross.

I see in Jesus One who is coming again – not "will come," but *is* coming – and is bringing with Him the City of God.

I see in Jesus the lover of my soul, who will never walk away from me.

I see in Jesus the centre of everything.

I see in Jesus my Lord and my God; I agree with Martin Luther: "I know of no God but this one in the manger."*

I see in Jesus the hope of the world.

I see in Jesus the future.

I see in Jesus the fundamental reason I want to go on living.

What do you see?

Prayer

Be near me, Lord Jesus,
I ask Thee to stay
Close by me forever, and love me I pray.
Bless all the dear children
in Thy tender care,
and fit us for heaven,
to live with Thee there.
Amen.

* As given in Norman E. Nagel, "Martinus: 'Heresy, Doctor Luther, Heresy!' The Person and Work of Christ," in *Seven-Headed Luther: Essays in Commemoration of a Quincentenary 1483-1983*, ed. Peter Newman Brooks (Oxford: Clarendon Press, 1983), 48.

If the Real Story Be Told . . .

One of the ironies of modern history is that the majority of people who celebrate around the Christmas story have never really heard the story! Oh, many have heard the basic story line. Many can even name some of the characters in the story line: Mary, Joseph, an angel named Gabriel, some shepherds, some wise men from the East, Caesar Augustus, Herod the King, and, of course, the infant Jesus. But the majority of those who benefit from the story line have never really heard the real story in the story line.

The story is told in narrative form by a tax collector named Matthew and a medical doctor named Luke. Churches regularly read portions of Luke's narrative on Christmas Eve. If you have not read the story recently, I encourage you to do so – Luke chapter 1, followed by Matthew chapter 1, followed by Luke chapter 2, and then Matthew chapter 2 – the story in narrative form.

The story is re-told in poetic form by a fisherman named John in the opening section of the Gospel that bears his name. John 1:1-18 is usually called the prologue to John, and it goes like this:

> In the beginning was the Word,
> and the Word was with God,
> and the Word was God.
> He was in the beginning with God.
> All things came into being through Him,
> and apart from Him
> nothing came into being
> that has come into being.
> In Him was life,
> and the life was the Light of men.
> The Light shines in the darkness,
> and the darkness did not comprehend it.
> There came a man sent from God,
> whose name was John.
> He came as a witness,
> to testify about the Light,
> so that all might believe through him.
> He was not the Light,
> but he came to testify about the Light.
> This was the true Light which,
> coming into the world,
> enlightens every man.
> He was in the world,
> and the world was made through Him,
> and the world did not know Him.
> He came to His own,
> and those who were His own
> did not receive Him.

But as many as received Him,
to them He gave the right
to become children of God,
even to those who believe in His name,
who were born,
not of blood
nor of the will of the flesh
nor of the will of man,
but of God.
And the Word became flesh,
and dwelt among us,
and we saw His glory,
glory as of the only begotten
from the Father,
full of grace and truth.
John testified about Him and cried out, saying,
"This was He of whom I said,
'He who comes after me
has a higher rank than I,
for He existed before me.'"
For of His fullness we have all received,
and grace upon grace.
For the Law was given through Moses;
grace and truth were realized
through Jesus Christ.
No one has seen God at any time;
the only begotten God
who is in the bosom of the Father,
He has explained Him.

Wow!

I have often wondered if any of the people who played a part in the story understood what was really happening. Did the angels who announced the birth even begin to grasp the magnitude of what was taking place in Bethlehem? Did the shepherds, who ran to the stable in response to the angel's announcement, realize how utterly appropriate it was for grown men to fall in adoration before the Baby? Did Mary, who gave birth to the Baby and held Him in her arms, know what had really taken place through her womb?

Luke tells us that after the shepherds left the manger scene, Mary "treasured up all these things, pondering them in her heart" (Luke 2:19). Did she get it? And if she did, how was she able to handle it?

This is what happened:

The One who made the world had entered the world in person!

The One who created the world had become a creature – a human being!

God became a man!

That is the real story that seldom surfaces in the holiday celebrations. That is the good news worth printing on the front page of every newspaper in the world. That is the arresting news that ought to be sweeping across the Internet tonight. Every person on the planet ought to hear the news at least once. Tweet it around the globe: "The Living God has become one of us!"

Now, I do not know about you, but all I can say is "unbelievable!" Not in the sense of "no way, not true," but in the sense sportscasters use the word: "Oh, wow! Never in my wildest imagination did I ever think *that* could happen! Did you see that? Unbelievable!"

That there is a God, a Living God, I cannot prove . . . but I can handle. That the Living God created this universe "out of nothing," I cannot prove . . . but I can handle. That the Living God did all kinds of miraculous deeds that the Bible claims God did, like parting the Red Sea . . . I can handle. I can get my mind around such deeds; I can imagine such things happening. But this? What the Living God did on Christmas Eve?

When Caesar Augustus was Emperor of Rome, and when a certain Quirinius was Governor of Syria, the Living God entered into the full orb of human existence . . . and did so as a Baby! "This will be a sign for you . . . you will find a Baby."

Have you ever heard anything so fantastic? The Creator became a creature! God became a man! Forgive me for saying it again, but "unbelievable!"

Do you see now why I said that most people who celebrate around the Christmas story have never really heard the story? Oh yes, most have heard about the special little Jewish boy born to a special Jewish couple on a starlit night. And yes, many have heard that the special little Jewish boy is claimed to be the long-awaited Jewish Messiah. Millions even flock to hear and sing Handel's "Messiah."

But most have not heard that the little Jewish boy was in fact, as Dorothy Sayers put it, "in the most exact and literal sense of the words, the God 'by whom all things were made.'"*

> In the beginning was the Word.
> And the Word was with God.
> And the Word was God.
> All things came into being by Him....
> And the Word became flesh ... and dwelt among us.

The Word "moved into the neighborhood" (The Message), and took up residence as one of us. Unbelievable!

The word John uses that we translate as "Word" is *logos*. It comes into the English language in words like "logic" and "logical." One is logical who lives by logic, who lives according to the *logos*.

Now, why does the fisherman use this word? Why begin his story about Jesus by calling Jesus the *Logos*? Why not use the term "Son"? John will make much of that term

---

* Dorothy Sayers, "The Greatest Drama Ever Staged" in *The Whimsical Christian: 18 Essays* (New York: Macmillan, 1978), 12.

in the rest of his Gospel. Why not use it in the opening poem?

> In the beginning was the Son.
> And the Son was with God.
> And the Son was God.
> All things came into being by Him. . . .
> And the Son became flesh . . . and dwelt among us.

Why not say it that way?

Or, why not use other titles people were using to refer to Jesus? Like Son of Man, or Messiah, or Lamb, or Lord?

> In the beginning was the Lord.
> And the Lord was with God.
> And the Lord was God.
> All things came into being by Him. . . .
> And the Lord became flesh . . . and dwelt among us.

Why not say it that way?

Because John wants to reach as wide an audience as possible. He wants to begin his story about Jesus on a note that will hook into as wide a scope of humanity as possible. And the word *logos* does that. *Logos* rings chords deep within every culture John knows.

Not that John is affirming everything every culture means when it uses the term *logos*, just that *logos* gives him an entry into the minds and hearts of the full scope of the humanity of his time. John ends up saying a whole lot more than anyone meant by *logos*. But this term enables him to meet people on common ground.

For example, the Greeks of John's day used the term *logos* a lot. For the philosopher Heraclitus, the *logos* is the rational principle behind the universe, the source of life, that which gives life its "reason-ableness." For the Stoic philosopher, the *logos* is the integrating principle behind the universe, that which makes the laws of nature, that which maintains nature and gives it unity and dynamism.

> In the beginning was the Rational-Integrating Principle.
> And the Rational-Integrating Principle was with God.
> And the Rational-Integrating Principle was God.
> All things came into being by Him. . . .
> And the Rational-Integrating Principle became flesh . . . and dwelt among us.

Whoa!

For the Jewish philosopher, Philo of Alexandria, the *logos* was "the agent of creation . . . the medium of divine government in the world."* Even though, for Philo, the *logos* is impersonal, he called the *logos* "the captain and pilot of the universe."†

---

* George R. Beasley-Murray, *John* (Waco: Word Books, 1987), 6.
† Ibid.

In the beginning was the Captain and Pilot of the Universe.

"I agree," says Philo.

And the Captain and the Pilot of the Universe was with God.

"I agree," says Philo.

And the Captain and Pilot of the Universe was God.

"What?" says Philo.

And the Captain and Pilot of the Universe became flesh . . . and dwelt among us.

"What?"

For most of the Jews of John's day, the *logos* is that by which the Living God communicates with humanity. The *logos* is not personal, by any means, but is the vehicle by which the Personal God communicates and creates. "In the beginning God created the heavens and the earth . . . and God said . . ." (Genesis 1). The *Logos*, the Word, is the means by which God acts in the world, creating (Psalm 33:6), revealing (the prophets often say, "the Word of the Lord came upon me"), and redeeming (Psalm 107:20; Isaiah 55:1). In short, the *Logos*, the Word, is God's way of expressing God's Self.

In the beginning was the Self-Expression.

And the Self-Expression was with God.

And the Self-Expression was God.

Of course, how could it be otherwise? God's Self-Expression can be nothing other than God's self! When we express ourselves, the expression is us. When the Living God expresses God's Self, the expression can be nothing other than, and nothing less than, God!

> In the beginning was the Self-Expression.
> And the Self-Expression was God.
> All things came into being by Him. . . .
> And the Self-Expression became flesh . . . and dwelt among us.

Unbelievable!

What if we had been chosen to write the prologue, the poem that tells the real story of Christmas? What term would we use that has affinities with *logos*? What about "Higher Power"? Now, we might not mean what everyone who uses it means, but it might be a good place to start.

> In the beginning was the Higher Power.
>   "OK," say the majority of people today.
>   And the higher Power was with God.
>   "OK, ok."
> And the Higher Power was God.
>   "Well . . ."
> All things came into being by Him.
>   "Him? Personal?"
> And the Higher Power became flesh . . . and dwelt among us.
>   "What?"

Or maybe we would use the term "Grand Unified Field Force."

> In the beginning was the Grand Unified Field Force.
> "Of course," the majority would say.
> And the Grand Unified Field Force was with God.
> "Well . . ."
> And the Grand Unified Field Force was God.
> "Whoa . . ."
> All things came into being by Him.
> "By Him? The Force is personal?"
> And the Grand Unified Field Force became flesh . . .
> and dwelt among us.
> "What?"

Unbelievable!

John began on this mind-boggling note to make sure that we read the rest of his story correctly. He wants us to realize that Mary's child, the Man from Galilee, who walks with, eats with, and plays with real flesh-and-blood people, is none other than the Maker of the Universe. The Man who laughs so hard that the religious establishment accuses Him of being drunk . . . the Man who weeps so deeply at the grave of his grown friend . . . is nothing other than "the Ground of all Being."

The Man who gets so tired and thirsty that He has to ask a Samaritan woman for a drink of water is the One who "in the beginning" made the first hydrogen and oxygen atoms, and determined that two hydrogen and one oxygen make water!

Nothing in all of human literature, nothing in all the myths by which we have sought to understand reality, can compare with the real Christmas story.

When Caesar Augustus thought he ruled the world, the One who spoke all the galaxies and all their stars into whirling space lay speechless in a cattle trough. When Quirinius was governor of Syria, the Star-Maker entrusted Himself to the care of a teenage girl. When Herod the Great was strutting his supposed power, God the *Logos* needed a mother to feed Him and change His diapers! Unbelievable!

The term theologians use for this grand miracle is "incarnation." It means "enfleshment." Christmas is all about the enfleshment of the Creator! And this is the sign: "You will find a baby lying in a manger." I have to say it again: Unbelievable!

Many people have tried to express the wonder of the real story. Saint Augustine of the fifth century tried:

> That Lord through whom all things were made (Jn 1:3), and who was himself made among all things; . . . the maker and placer of the sun, made and placed under the sun; . . . producer of heaven and earth, appearing on earth under heaven; unspeakably wise, wisely speechless as an infant.

Saint Ephrem the Syriac of the fourth century tried:

> The Word entered her [Mary], and became silent within her; thunder entered her, and His voice was still; the Shepherd of all entered her; He became a Lamb in her.

Charles Wesley of the eighteenth century tried:

> Veiled in flesh the Godhead see,
> Hail the incarnate Deity.
> Pleased as man with us to dwell,
> Jesus, our Emmanuel.

C.S. Lewis of the twentieth century tried:

> In our world too, a Stable once had something inside it that was bigger than our whole world.

Sonny Salsbury has tried:

> Those hands that formed the universe,
> created you and me,
> have now come down in human form ...
> for us God's love to see ...
> Come and see the five little fingers of God.

Keith Getty and Stuart Townend of Ireland have tried:

> Hands that set each star in place,
> Shaped the earth in darkness,

Cling now to a mother's breast,
Vuln'rable and helpless.

Margaret Clarkson of Canada has tried:

Lord of the universe, hope of the world,
Lord of the limitless reaches of space,
Here on this planet You put on our flesh,
Vastness confined in the womb of a maid,
Born in our likeness you ransomed our race.
. . .
Lord of the universe, hope of the world,
Lord of the infinite eons of time,
You came among us, lived our brief years,
Tasted our griefs, our aloneness, our fears,
conquered our death, made eternity ours.

Luci Shaw has tried. She has Mary say:

Quiet he lies
whose vigor hurled
a universe. He sleeps
whose eyelids have not closed before. . . .
Older than eternity, now he
is new. Now native to earth as I am, nailed
to my poor planet, caught that I might be free,
blind in my womb to know my darkness ended,
brought to this birth
for me to be new-born,
and for him to see me mended,
I must see him torn.

Unbelievable. Simply unbelievable!

The implications of the real story are many . . . and staggering! Let me name just a few of them.

First, if the real story be told, we humans have been granted unbelievable dignity. Our flesh and blood have been granted royal dignity. God did not become an angel. God did not become an eagle, or a moose, or a whale. God became a human being, forever dignifying our bodily existence. God so loved us that God became us. Us!

Second, if the real story be told, we discover the unbelievable depth of God's love. God so loved us that God changed! God altered the mode of His being. Before Christmas, the Living God was pure spirit – all three persons of the Trinity, pure spirit. In the Incarnation, One of the Three – the second person of the Trinity – changed His mode of Being, taking up our humanity, changing the form of the relationships within God. God became what God was not!

As cute as penguins are, I would never become a penguin to help penguins out of their predicament. As majestic as whales are, I would not become a whale to help whales out of their predicament. For that would mean becoming what I am not at a fundamental level.

God became what God was not! God the *Logos* changed the form of His existence forever so that we might be freed from all that keeps us from being fully human. The unbelievable depth of the Creator's love!

Third, if the real story be told, we have unbelievable comfort in our suffering. Christmas expresses the unbelievable empathy of God. Most humans who believe in God believe that God is aware of our pain. But many wonder if God feels our pain. God might sympathize, but can God empathize? "The Word became flesh . . . ." God became humanity-in-pain. God became humanity-in-grief.

Songwriter Sydney Carter (author of "Lord of the Dance") imagines the thief who was crucified on the cross next to Jesus speaking to Jesus:

> It's God they ought to crucify
> Instead of you and me.
> I said to the carpenter
> A-hanging on the tree.*

"I wish the carpenter had made the world," I said to the carpenter a-hanging on the tree. But what does the real Christmas story proclaim? The carpenter did make the world! God was a-hanging on the tree. God knows first-hand what it means to be human in a violent, unjust world. Indeed, no one knows human suffering more than the "humanized" God.

* Sydney Carter, "Friday Morning," written 1960.

Fourth, if the real story be told, we have unbelievable hope for the future. We have unbelievable certainty that we shall be made whole. For in the stable on Christmas Eve, God forever wedded Himself to our humanity. God forever tied up His future with our future. The future of humanity is as secure as the future of God! The enfleshed God is the guarantee that one day all flesh will be fully redeemed. Jesus would later say, "Because I live, you will live also" (John 14:19).

Fifth, if the real story be told, the unbelievable claims of Jesus have unbelievable believability. If Jesus, Mary's boy, is indeed the Living God in our humanity, then it is quite logical, quite rational, for Him to claim what no mere human can claim.

Of course He can say, "I am the bread of life."

Of course He can say, "I am the light of the world."

Of course He can say, "I am the way, the truth, the life."

Of course He can say, "Before Abraham was, I am."

Of course He can say, "If you are thirsty, come to me and drink and out of your innermost being will flow rivers of living water."

If Mary's boy is the God to whom we must all give an account for our lives, and He says, "Your sins are forgiven," then they are forgiven!

If Mary's boy is the Creator wrapped in our flesh, when He cries out from the cross "It is finished," it is finished!

If He is the Almighty come to earth as one of us, and He says to us, "Follow Me," we can be sure He knows where He is going . . . and we can be sure that following Him is the smartest thing anyone can do!

Sixth, if the real story be told, we realize how unbelievably right it was for shepherds to fall down before the Baby and worship Him. If the real story be told, we realize how unbelievably right it was for wise men from the east to leave their work, spend their time and money crossing the Arabian Desert, and then fall to their knees before the Child and worship Him. If the real story be told, we realize how unbelievably right it is for millions upon millions of people in every corner of the globe to follow the lead of the shepherds and wise men and worship Jesus.

A favourite Christmas card says it best:

The Word did not become a philosophy to be discussed, a theory to be debated, a concept to be pondered. The Word became a Person to be followed, enjoyed, and loved!

One more time:

> In the beginning was the Logos.
> And the Logos was with God.
> And the Logos was God.
> And the Logos became what we are . . . flesh.
> God became a man.

Unbelievable.

The Most Wonderful Time of All Years

Let all mortal flesh keep silence
And with fear and trembling stand.
Ponder nothing earthly minded,
For with blessing in His hand.
Christ our God to earth descendeth,
Our full homage to demand.[*]

* "Let All Mortal Flesh Keep Silence." Words from the Liturgy of St. James, 4th century; trans. Gerard Moultrie.

CPSIA information can be obtained
at www.ICGtesting.com
Printed in the USA
BVOW08s1445241017
498520BV00001B/13/P